THE 100+ SERIES™

Reproducible Activities

M000036234

Using the Standards
Number & Operations

Grade 1

By
Becky Daniel

Published by Instructional Fair • TS Denison
an imprint of

Mc Graw Hill **Children's Publishing**

Author: Becky Daniel-White
Editor: Rebecca Warren, Melissa Warner Hale

Published by Instructional Fair • TS Denison
An imprint of McGraw-Hill Children's Publishing
Copyright © 2003 McGraw-Hill Children's Publishing

Send all inquiries to:
McGraw-Hill Children's Publishing
3195 Wilson Drive NW
Grand Rapids, Michigan 49544

Using the Standards: Number & Operations—grade 1
ISBN: 0-7424-1811-1

1 2 3 4 5 6 7 8 9 PHXBK 08 07 06 05 04 03

The McGraw-Hill Companies

Table of Contents

Introduction

Youngsters are naturally active and resourceful. They will construct, modify, and integrate ideas by interacting with the physical world. At play, they begin to form connections that clarify and extend concepts introduced in the classroom. Games that incorporate mathematical terms will provide concrete models and help students to develop number sense.

By the first grade, children have acquired a wide range of individual mathematics understanding; therefore, their level of knowledge must be appropriately assessed. Interviews and observations will be your best guide. It is recommended that the Pretest/Post Test, found on pages 7 and 8, be presented at the beginning and end of each chapter.

For easy record keeping, a checklist of skills is provided at the end of each chapter (pages 54, 79, and 117). When compiled, the three-page skills checklist will provide you with a comprehensive mathematical continuum for your first graders. A file folder containing each student's tests and checklists should be kept for easy access.

The first chapter, **Number Systems,** provides practice in understanding numbers, the ways of representing numbers, and the relationships among numbers. Counting 1 to 100 is introduced, as students have the opportunity to recognize multiple representations of each number (numeral, base-ten blocks, and number word). Comparing numbers using greater than and less than is another way students begin to understand how numbers relate to each other.

Chapter 2, **Operations,** explores the meaning of adding and subtracting as individual operations. Students understand that adding means making more and subtracting means making less. It also makes connections to the relationships between operations, such as opposite problems of addition and subtraction $(3 + 2 = 5$ and $5 - 2 = 3)$.

The last chapter, **Computation,** will help students develop and use strategies for computations. Number pairs for addition and subtraction, methods and tools to solve mathematical problems, and mental computations (estimating) are all included.

The 100+ activity sheets herein were developed in accordance with standards as prescribed by the National Council of Teachers of Mathematics. Each of the three chapters—Number Systems, Operations, and Computation—is based on one of the three major content strands for Numbers and Operations. Each chapter also contains a sampling of the five process strands for mathematics:

- Problem Solving
- Connections
- Reasoning and Proof
- Representation
- Communication

4

Look for the icons at the top of each page to see which process strands are covered by that activity. Or check the Correlation to NCTM Standards chart on page 6 for a listing of page numbers by process strand.

In the early grades, building mathematical knowledge through **problem solving** should involve situations that arise in the classroom. Example: We have 23 students in our class, and there are 24 cookies in this box. Are there enough for everyone to have a cookie? Will we have any extra cookies? How many will be left over?

Reasoning and proof are fundamental aspects of mathematics that require young learners to make assumptions and to investigate whether their ideas are sound. A variety of manipulatives can be used as students practice adding more objects and taking away objects to test addition and subtraction problems.

Language is as important to learning mathematics as it is when learning to read. In order to make assumptions and test ideas, students must be able to **communicate** their thoughts. In the classroom, it is important that youngsters hear the language of mathematics in meaningful context. To optimize mathematical thinking, create and structure a mathematically rich environment for your students. Exploring their ideas will give your students practice in thinking coherently and communicating ideas clearly to peers, teachers, and others. Organizing and consolidating mathematical thinking through communication can be as casual as, "Tomorrow is David's birthday. How many days does he have to wait to celebrate?" Model appropriate conventional vocabulary and when necessary, encourage students to make and use the vocabulary cards at the back of this book to practice using mathematical language.

When students learn to make assumptions, test their assumptions, and discuss them coherently, they will be able to recognize and use **connections** among mathematical ideas and to the world around them. Is there another way of saying "Six comes between 5 and 7"? (Six is one more than five and one less than seven. Six is the same as 5 + 1 and 7 – 1.)

As students begin to create and use **representations** to organize, record, and communicate mathematical ideas, they will be able to solve complicated problems and make predictions. Even very young children can be taught to use models to understand physical, social, and mathematical phenomena.

When students are taught to problem solve, reason to prove, communicate mathematical ideas, make connections, and use representation to interpret mathematical phenomena, math will become more than simply numbers and operations. Mathematics will become the key to understanding their universe and how everything in it relates to everything else.

McGraw-Hill Children's Publishing

Correlation to NCTM Standards

	Problem Solving	Reasoning and Proof	Communication	Connections	Representation
Number Systems	10, 18, 20, 21, 23, 24, 30, 31, 32, 33, 34, 35, 36, 50	11, 12, 13, 19, 28, 29, 42, 43, 45, 46, 47, 48, 49	9, 16, 17, 18, 21, 22, 26, 27, 28, 29, 30, 32, 35, 40, 41, 42, 43, 44, 45, 50	14, 15, 16, 17, 23, 24, 25, 26, 27, 31, 33, 36, 37, 38, 39, 40, 41	9, 10, 11, 12, 13, 14, 15, 16, 17, 19, 20, 22, 23, 24, 25, 28, 33, 37, 38, 39, 44, 46, 47, 48, 49, 50, 52, 53
Operations	52, 53, 54, 56, 57, 59, 60, 62, 64, 65, 66, 68, 69, 70, 71, 72, 73, 74, 75, 78	55, 60, 61, 62, 63, 64, 67, 74, 75	56, 65, 69	52, 53, 54, 55, 58, 59, 61, 62, 63, 64, 66, 67, 68, 69, 70, 73, 74, 75, 76, 77	54, 58, 61, 65, 71, 73, 76, 77, 78
Computation	81, 85, 87, 88, 90, 93, 96, 97, 99, 101, 102, 103, 104, 105, 106, 107, 109, 111, 112, 113, 114, 115, 116	80, 82, 83, 84, 86, 91, 95, 98, 100, 106, 108, 110, 111, 113	87, 88, 100, 103, 104, 106 109, 114, 115, 116	80, 89, 92, 97 105, 108, 111, 112	80, 81, 82, 83, 84, 86, 89, 90, 91, 92, 93, 94, 95, 98, 100, 102, 103, 107, 108,

0-7424-1811-1 *Number & Operation*

Name _____ Date _____

Pretest/Post Test

1. Circle the even numbers.

2   5   8   11   18   20

2. Circle the odd numbers.

2   6   9   11   15   21

3. Counting by 2s, what number comes after 16? _____

4. Counting by 5s, what comes after 60? _____

5. Counting by 10s, what number comes after 70? _____

6. Write the number for each of these words.

one _____   forty-five _____

twenty _____   ninety-eight _____

7. Write the number that comes after.

8 _____   31 _____   65 _____

8. Write the number that comes before.

_____ 1   _____ 48   _____ 97

9. Use a picture and word to show each number two more ways.

27 _____   14 _____

McGraw-Hill Children's Publishing   0-7424-1811-1 *Number & Operations*

Pretest/Post Test

10. Use the sign **>**, **<**, or **=** to complete the number sentences.

5 ⬚ 8   11 ⬚ 9   15 ⬚ 15

11. Color the part of the shape that matches each fraction.

$\frac{1}{3}$  $\frac{1}{2}$  $\frac{1}{4}$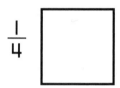

12. Write the number that will continue the patterns.

2   4   6   8   10   12   14   16 _____

5   10   15   20   25   30   35   40 _____

13. Circle the first animal. Cross out the last animal. Draw a box around the second animal. Draw a triangle around the third animal.

14. Find the sums.

   a. 3 + 1 = _____

   b. 1 + 6 = _____

   c. 2 + 5 = _____

15. Find the differences.

   a. 5 − 3 = _____

   b. 8 − 2 = _____

   c. 9 − 1 = _____

16. On the back of this sheet, write the numbers as far as you can count.

0-7424-1811-1 *Number & Operation*

Name _____ Date _____

One to Twelve

Directions: Count the objects. Write the number on the line.

1.   _____

2.   _____

3.  _____

4.   _____

5.   _____

6.   _____

Do More: Take turns counting out loud. Count objects in the room. How many rows of desks? How many desks in each row? How many pencils? How many books?

McGraw-Hill Children's Publishing   0-7424-1811-1 *Number & Operations*

How Many?

Directions: Count the number of each kind of animal. Write the total on the line.

How many?

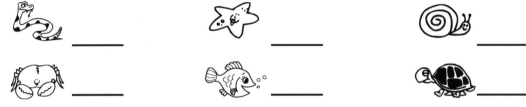

Do More: Find the mystery animal in the picture. It is an animal not shown at the top. What is the best way to locate the mystery animal?

0-7424-1811-1 *Number & Operation*

Name _____ Date _____

Guess How Many

Directions: Guess how many of each kind of ball is in the picture. Do not count yet. Write your guess on the first line. Then count the balls. Write how many on the line. How close was your guess?

Guess   **How many?**

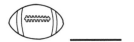   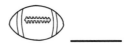

   ___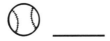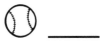

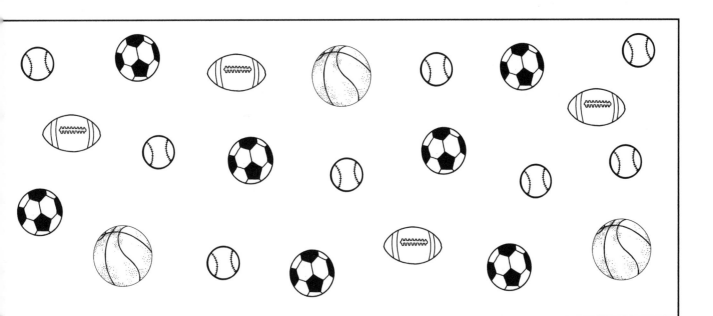

Do More: Draw a counting picture with different kinds of balls. Trade pictures with a friend. Count each kind of ball in your friend's picture.

11

Name _____ Date _____

Number Words

Directions: Cut and paste each number word in the right box.

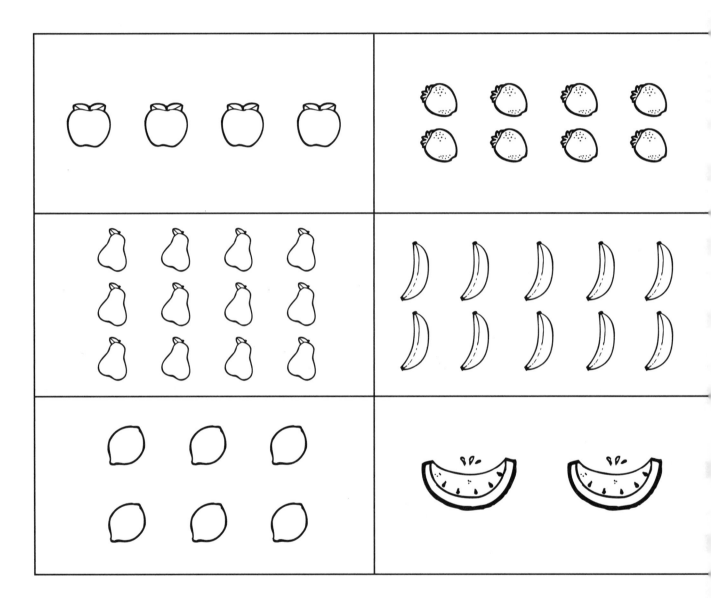

| two | four | six | eight | ten | twelve |

0-7424-1811-1 *Number & Operation*

Name _____ Date _____

Matching

Directions: Draw a line to connect each set of dots with the number and matching number word. The first one has been done for you.

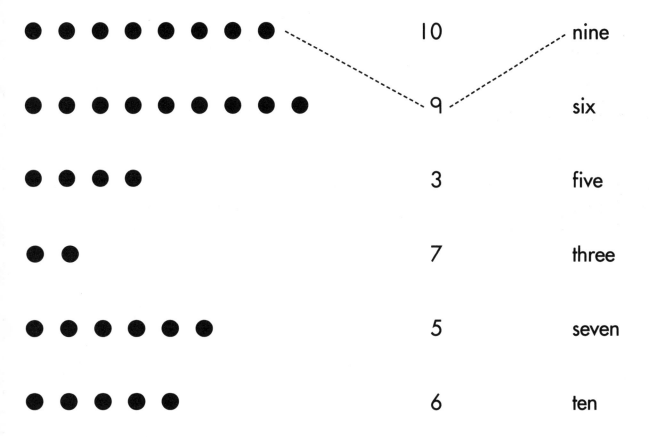

Do More: Make flash cards using the vocabulary cards in the back of the book. Use the number cards to practice matching number words.

McGraw-Hill Children's Publishing   0-7424-1811-1 *Number & Operations*

Name _____   Date _____

Ten to a Cage

Directions: Draw a cage around each set of 10 animals.
Find the total of each kind of animal.

1.

2.

3.

4.

Do More: The set of 10 animals is written with the numeral 1 (for 1 set of 10) in the tens column. The leftover animals represent the number in the ones column. Tell how many tens and how many ones for each problem on this page.

0-7424-1811-1 *Number & Operation*

Name _____ Date _____

Three Ways (1-20)

There is more than one way to show a number.
A number can be a **numeral,** a **word,** or a **picture**.

I2	twelve	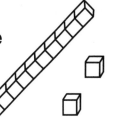
numeral	**word**	**picture**

Directions: Show each number 3 different ways.

1. numeral _____6_____

   word _____

   picture

2. numeral _____

   word ___twelve___

   picture

3. numeral ___I3___

   word _____

   picture

4. numeral _____

   word ___eleven___

   picture

0-7424-1811-1 *Number & Operations*

Name _____ Date _____

Greater Than, Less Than (1-20)

The hungry mouth always opens to more!
Use **>** for **greater than** and **<** for **less than.**

 2 < 4   4 > 2

Two is **less than** four.   Four is **greater than** two.

Directions: Greater than or less than? Put the right sign in each row.

1.   7 ☐ 4

2.   5 ☐ 12 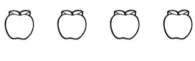

3.   16 ☐ 3 

4.   12 ☐ 20

Do More: Take turns saying each equation out loud. Use complete sentences. Example: Seven apples is greater than four apples.

0-7424-1811-1 *Number & Operation*

Name _____ Date _____

Greater Than, Less Than (1-20)

Use > for **greater than** and < for **less than**.

  <   **>**

Two cents is less than ten cents.   Ten cents is greater than eight cents.

 = 1¢   = 5¢    = 10¢

Directions: Write how many cents. Which side has more money? Fill in a greater than (**>**) or less than (**<**) sign.

1.   ☐

2.   ☐

3.   ☐

4.   ☐

Do More: Use pennies, nickels, and dimes to make a new equation. Have a friend tell which sign should be used—greater than or less than.

17

0-7424-1811-1 *Number & Operations*

Name _____   Date _____

The Twenties

Directions: What numbers come after 19? The twenties! Write the number that comes after each number given. Use the number chart to help you.

21 _____   23 _____

19 _____   24 _____

27 _____   20 _____

22 _____   25 _____

28 _____   26 _____

1	2	3	4	5	6	7	8	9	10
11	12	13	14	15	16	17	18	19	20
21	22	23	24	25	26	27	28	29	30

Do More: Play "What Comes Next?" with a friend. One person says a number and then the other tells the number that follows.

0-7424-1811-1 *Number & Operation*

Name _____ Date _____

Domino Totals

Directions: Guess the number of dots on each set of dominoes. Write your guess on the first line. Then count the dots on each set of dominoes. Write the total on the line. How close was your guess?

1.

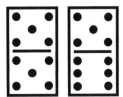

Guess _____

How many? _____

2.

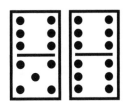

Guess _____

How many? _____

3.

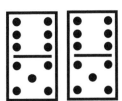

Guess _____

How many? _____

4.

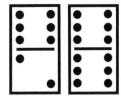

Guess _____

How many? _____

5.

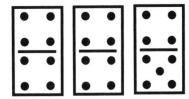

Guess _____

How many? _____

6.

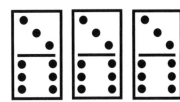

Guess _____

How many? _____

Do More: Use dominoes to show the totals for the numbers 13 to 30. Draw sets of dominoes showing a total of 30.

0-7424-1811-1 *Number & Operations*

Name _____ Date _____

The Thirties

Directions: Every number in the thirties will have 3 sets of 10. Draw the right number of squares in each set. Put a circle around each set of 10 squares. The first one has been done for you.

30	33
□□□□□□□□□□ (circled) □□□□□□□□□□ (circled) □□□□□□□□□□ (circled)	
36	**34**
37	**39**

Do More: Use base-ten cubes to represent each number on this page.

0-7424-1811-1 *Number & Operation*

Name _____ Date _____

Forties and Fifties

Directions: Complete the number chart to count all the way through the forties and fifties. How fast can you go?

1	2	____	4	5	6	7	8	9	____
11	12	13	14	15	16	17	18	____	20
21	____	23	24	____	26	27	____	29	30
31	32	____	34	____	36	____	38	39	40
41	____	43	____	45	____	47	____	49	50
51	____	53	____	____	56	____	58	____	60

Do More: Use a stopwatch to see how long it takes to count to 60. Who can count to 60 the fastest? Who can write the numbers 1 to 60 in less than 3 minutes? How far can you count in 60 seconds?

0-7424-1811-1 *Number & Operations*

Name _____ Date _____

Connecting Numerals

Directions: Draw a line to connect the matching numerals and the number words. The first one has been done for you.

1.	59	thirty-two
2.	47	fifty-nine
3.	32	forty-seven
4.	61	twenty-eight
5.	53	fifty-three
6.	28	sixty-one
7.	25	fifty-five
8.	44	nineteen
9.	19	forty-four
10.	55	twenty-five

Do More: Find a friend. Say a number from the right column out loud. Your friend writes the correct numeral. Take turns.

0-7424-1811-1 *Number & Operation*

Name _____ Date _____

Sheep for Sale

 = $1  = $10

Directions: White sheep cost $1. Black sheep cost $10. In each row, write the total value of the sheep. The first one has been done for you.

1.  $13

2.  _____

3.   _____

4.    _____

5.        _____

Do More: Write an addition problem to explain how you found the total value of the sheep.

  0-7424-1811-1 *Number & Operations*

Name _____ Date _____

Lion's Share

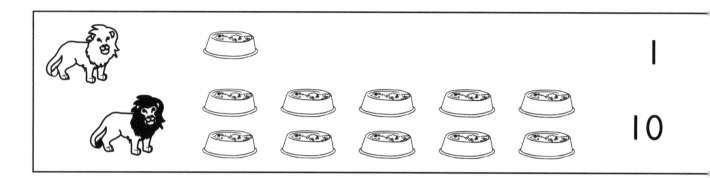

Directions: Lions with white manes eat 1 tub of food every day. Lions with black manes eat 10 tubs of food every day. How much food is needed in each row? Draw a picture to help you solve the problem.

1. _____ 14 tubs of food

2. _____

3. _____

4. _____

5. _____

Do More: Explain how you solved the problem to a friend.

0-7424-1811-1 *Number & Operation*

Name _____ Date _____

Three Ways (21-50)

There is more than one way to show a number.
A number can be a **numeral,** a **word,** or a **picture**.

34	thirty-four	
numeral	**word**	**picture**

Directions: Show each number 3 different ways.

1. numeral _____40_____

word _____

picture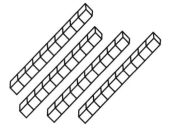

2. numeral _____

word __twenty-one__

picture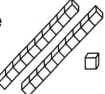

3. numeral ____37____

word _____

picture

4. numeral _____

word __eleven__

picture

25

0-7424-1811-1 *Number & Operations*

Name _____ Date _____

Greater Than, Less Than *(21-50)*

> slide down   < climb up
  1 number   1 number

Directions: To complete each sentence, choose the number that is 1 **greater than** or **less than** the number listed. Be sure to check the sign before you pick a number! The first one has been done for you

1.   34 > ☐

2.   41 < ☐

3.   26 < ☐

4.   55 > ☐

5.   39 < ☐

6.   45 < ☐

Do More: Share your problems with a friend. Take turns saying the problem out loud: Thirty-four is greater than thirty-three.

0-7424-1811-1 *Number & Operations*

Name _____ Date _____

Greater Than, Less Than, or Equal? (21-50)

42 > 25	31 < 56	38 = 38
Use **>** for **greater than**.	Use **<** for **less than**.	Use **=** for **equal**.

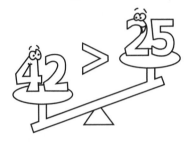  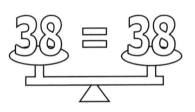

Directions: Fill in each box with the correct sign—greater than, less than, or equal.

1. 33 ☐ 50

2. 27 ☐ 44

3. 48 ☐ 26

4. 21 ☐ 21

5. 49 ☐ 38

6. 34 ☐ 45

Do More: Say each equation out loud using words: Forty-two is greater than twenty-five. Thirty-eight is equal to thirty-eight.

 0-7424-1811-1 *Number & Operations*

Name _____ Date _____

Even and Odd Numbers

Directions: Which are the **even** numbers? Start at number 2. Use a red crayon to circle every other number. Which are the **odd** numbers? Start at number 1. Use a blue crayon to put an X over every other number. To prove your work, be sure the red circles and the blue Xs are lined up in columns.

1	2	3	4	5	6	7	8	9	10
11	12	13	14	15	16	17	18	19	20
21	22	23	24	25	26	27	28	29	30
31	32	33	34	35	36	37	38	39	40
41	42	43	44	45	46	47	48	49	50
51	52	53	54	55	56	57	58	59	60
61	62	63	64	65	66	67	68	69	70
71	72	73	74	75	76	77	78	79	80
81	82	83	84	85	86	87	88	89	90
91	92	93	94	95	96	97	98	99	100

Do More: Use the chart to count the numbers from 1 to 100 out loud.

0-7424-1811-1 *Number & Operation*

Name _____ Date _____

Counting by Twos

Directions: Another way of counting by even numbers is counting by twos. Fill in the missing numbers.

1	___	3	___	5	___	7	___	9	___
11	___	13	___	15	___	17	___	19	___
21	___	23	___	25	___	27	___	29	___
31	___	33	___	35	___	37	___	39	___
41	___	43	___	45	___	47	___	49	___
51	___	53	___	55	___	57	___	59	___
61	___	63	___	65	___	67	___	69	___
71	___	73	___	75	___	77	___	79	___
81	___	83	___	85	___	87	___	89	___
91	___	93	___	95	___	97	___	99	___

Do More: Count out loud by twos from 2 to 100 (even numbers). Then count out loud by twos from 1 to 99 (odd numbers).

0-7424-1811-1 *Number & Operations*

Name _____ Date _____

What's the Missing Number?

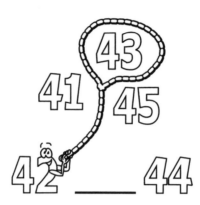

Directions: In each group, write the missing number on the line.

1.   6 _____ 8   **2.**   62 _____ 64

3.   20 _____ 22   **4.**   94 _____ 96

5.   9 _____ 11   **6.**   85 _____ 87

7.   32 _____ 34   **8.**   91 _____ 93

Do More: Find a friend. Name an even number. Your friend tells the next even number that follows. Then have your friend name an odd number. You tell the next odd number that follows.

   0-7424-1811-1 *Number & Operation*

Name _____ Date _____

Even or Odd?

Directions: All even numbers end with 0, 2, 4, 6, or 8. All odd numbers end with 1, 3, 5, 7, or 9. Use the code to color the design. All the even numbers will be red. All the odd numbers will be blue.

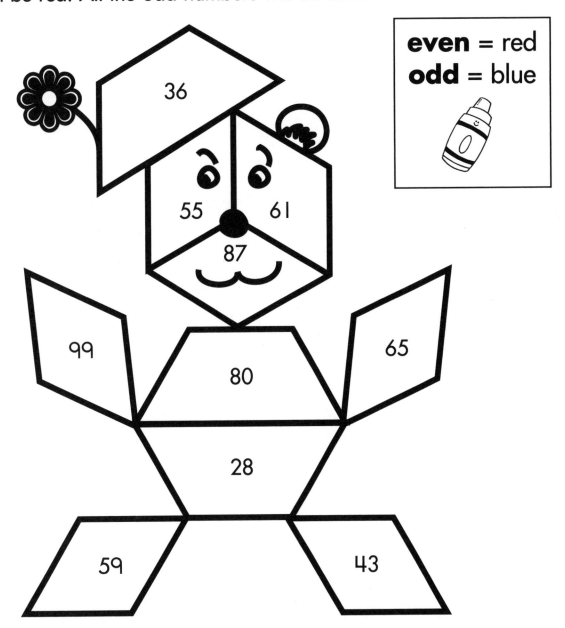

even = red
odd = blue

36
55 61
87
99 80 65
28
59 43

Do More: Use red and blue pattern blocks to match the shapes on the pattern.

0-7424-1811-1 *Number & Operations*

Name _____ Date _____

Counting by Fives

Directions: Circle every number that ends with a 5 or a 0. Watch the pattern that develops. The first row has been done for you.

1	2	3	4	(5)	6	7	8	9	(10)
11	12	13	14	15	16	17	18	19	20
21	22	23	24	25	26	27	28	29	30
31	32	33	34	35	36	37	38	39	40
41	42	43	44	45	46	47	48	49	50
51	52	53	54	55	56	57	58	59	60
61	62	63	64	65	66	67	68	69	70
71	72	73	74	75	76	77	78	79	80
81	82	83	84	85	86	87	88	89	90
91	92	93	94	95	96	97	98	99	100

Do More: Use this page to help you count out loud from 5 to 100.

0-7424-1811-1 *Number & Operation*

Name _____ Date _____

Counting by Tens

5 dimes   2 dimes
50¢   20¢

Directions: Use the dimes on this page to help you count by tens. How many dimes are there? How many cents total?

1.   _____ dimes   _____ ¢

2.
   _____ dimes   _____ ¢

3.   _____ dimes   _____ ¢

4.
          _____ dimes   _____ ¢

5.   _____ dimes   _____ ¢

0-7424-1811-1 *Number & Operations*

Name _____ Date _____

Counting to 100 Chart

Directions: Can you count to 100? Complete the chart by filling in the missing numbers.

1	2	3	___	5	___	7	___	9	___
11	___	___	___	___	___	17	___	19	___
21	___	___	___	25	___	___	___	___	30
31	32	33	___	___	___	37	___	39	___
41	___	43	___	45	___	47	___	___	50
51	___	___	___	55	___	57	___	59	___
___	62	___	___	___	66	___	___	69	___
___	___	73	___	75	76	___	___	___	80
81	___	83	___	___	___	87	___	89	___
___	___	93	94	95	___	___	___	___	___

0-7424-1811-1 *Number & Operations*

Name _____ Date _____

What Comes Before?

Directions: On each line, write the numeral that comes before each number.

_____ 45   _____ 50

_____ 66   _____ 73

_____ 99   _____ 16

_____ 89   _____ 100

_____ 61   _____ 82

_____ 78   _____ 93

_____ 33   _____ 24

Do More: Play "What Comes Before?" Give a number between 1 and 100. A friend tells the number that comes just before it.

© McGraw-Hill Children's Publishing   0-7424-1811-1 *Number & Operations*

Name _____ Date _____

Number Patterns

Directions: In each row, the numbers follow a pattern. Find the pattern and write the next two numbers.

1.	2	4	6	8	10	_____ _____
2.	5	10	15	20	25	_____ _____
3.	10	20	30	40	50	_____ _____
4.	1	3	5	7	9	_____ _____
5.	40	50	60	70	80	_____ _____

Do More: Make your own number pattern. Trade with a friend. What numbers come next in the pattern?

0-7424-1811-1 *Number & Operation*

Name _____ Date _____

Bean Poles

43  ⟋

There are **4 tens** in 43.   There are **3 ones** in 43.

Directions: Show the amount by drawing ten beans on each pole. Extra beans are drawn separately. How many tens? How many ones?

1. 37   **tens** _____ **ones** _____

2. 68   **tens** _____ **ones** _____

3. 55   **tens** _____ **ones** _____

4. 46   **tens** _____ **ones** _____

Do More: Make your own bean poles. Glue 10 beans to a craft stick. Each stick show the tens place. Use extra beans to show the ones place.

0-7424-1811-1 *Number & Operations*

Name _____ Date _____

Ones and Tens

32

tens	ones
3	2

Directions: In a 2-digit number, the first digit shows the **tens.** The second digit shows the **ones.** Write the correct digit in the tens and ones place for each number below.

1. 56

tens	ones

4. 64

tens	ones

2. 23

tens	ones

5. 95

tens	ones

3. 80

tens	ones

6. 48

tens	ones

Do More: Call out 2-digit numbers. Have a friend tell which digit shows the tens and which digit shows the ones.

0-7424-1811-1 *Number & Operations*

Name _____ Date _____

Three Ways (51-100)

There is more than one way to show a number.
A number can be a **numeral,** a **word,** or a **picture**.

68	sixty-eight	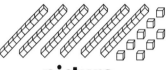
numeral	**word**	**picture**

Directions: Show each number 3 different ways.

I. numeral __55__

word _____

picture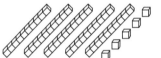

2. numeral _____

word **seventy-two**

picture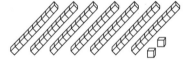

3. numeral __87__

word _____

picture

4. numeral __64__

word _____

picture

© McGraw-Hill Children's Publishing

0-7424-1811-1 *Number & Operations*

Name _____ Date _____

Greater Than, Less Than, or Equal? (51-100)

90 > 68	71 < 81	56 = 56
Use **>** for **greater than.**	Use **<** for **less than.**	Use **=** for **equal.**

Directions: Fill in each box with the correct sign—greater than, less than, or equal.

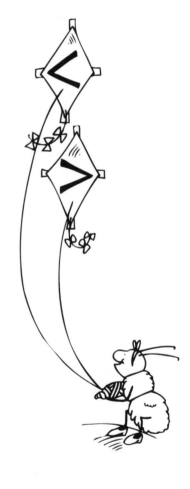

1. 81 ☐ 89

2. 37 ☐ 44

3. 67 ☐ 58

4. 75 ☐ 75

5. 32 ☐ 43

6. 96 ☐ 95

Do More: Play "Which Is More, Which Is Less?" Which is more: 67 or 89? Which is less: 88 or 54? Which is more: 58 or 85? Which is less: 99 or 89?

0-7424-1811-1 *Number & Operations*

Number Systems

Name _____ Date _____

Greater Than, Less Than, or Equal? (51-100)

Use 🧀 for **greater than.**   Use 🧀 for **less than.**

Directions: Circle the cheese with the correct sign.

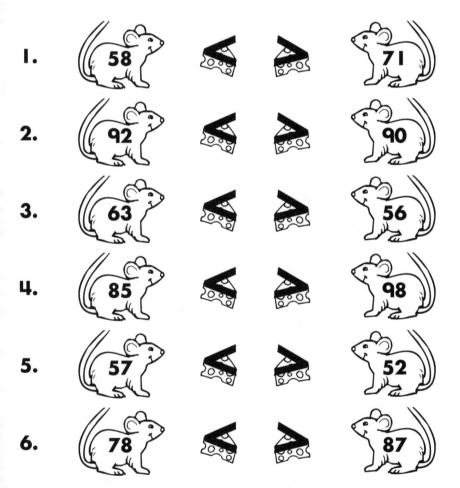

1. 58 < > 71

2. 92 < > 90

3. 63 < > 56

4. 85 < > 98

5. 57 < > 52

6. 78 < > 87

Do More: Play this game. Name 2 things. Tell which is greater.
Examples: Which is greater in number—days in a month or months in a year?
Inches in a yard or inches in a foot?

41

© McGraw-Hill Children's Publishing   0-7424-1811-1 *Number & Operations*

Name _____ Date _____

First and Last

Directions: In each row, color the first animal purple and the last animal orange.

Do More: Play "Follow the Leader." Tell who is first and last in line. Change leaders by having the last person go to the front of the line. Now who is first? Who is last? Who is next to the last?

0-7424-1811-1 *Number & Operation*

Name _____ Date _____

Second, Third, Fourth

Directions: Number the children in line. Match each child to the word that tells where he or she is in line.

third

first

second

fourth

Think: How else could you describe the fourth child in line on this page? How about the third child in line?

McGraw-Hill Children's Publishing

0-7424-1811-1 *Number & Operations*

Name _____ Date _____

Fifth to Tenth

Directions: Number the fingers. Follow the directions to color on the fifth through tenth fingers.

Put a blue ring on the **seventh** finger.
Draw a star on the **ninth** finger.
Color the **eighth** finger green.
Make a smile face on the **sixth** finger.
Color the **tenth** finger purple.

Do More: Trace your hands. Trade drawings with a friend. Give each other directions to color each finger. Hold up all 10 fingers and count out first, second, third, fourth, fifth, sixth, seventh, eighth, ninth, and tenth.

0-7424-1811-1 *Number & Operation*

Name _____ Date _____

First to Tenth

Directions: Follow the directions to color the elephants.

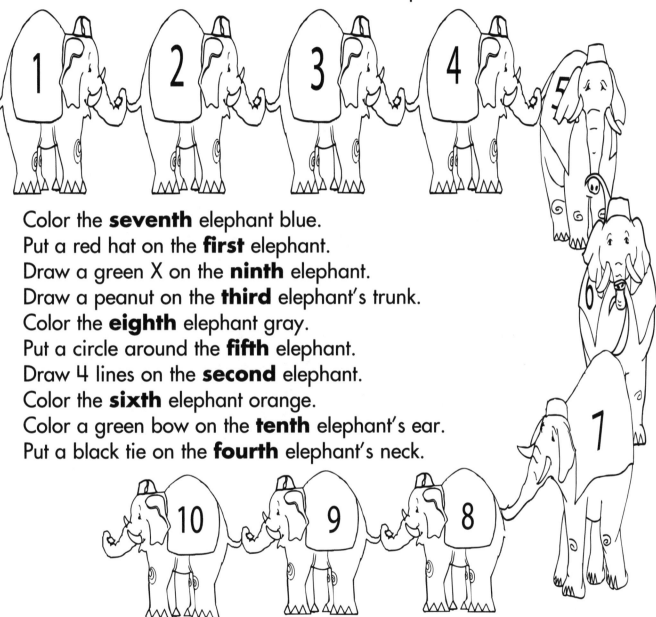

Color the **seventh** elephant blue.
Put a red hat on the **first** elephant.
Draw a green X on the **ninth** elephant.
Draw a peanut on the **third** elephant's trunk.
Color the **eighth** elephant gray.
Put a circle around the **fifth** elephant.
Draw 4 lines on the **second** elephant.
Color the **sixth** elephant orange.
Color a green bow on the **tenth** elephant's ear.
Put a black tie on the **fourth** elephant's neck.

Do More: Write the numbers 1 to 10, each on a separate piece of paper. Mix up the papers. Find 10 friends and give each a number. Arrange yourselves in line according to your number. Tell what place you are in line.

0-7424-1811-1 *Number & Operations*

Name _____   Date _____

One Half

Directions: Color one half ($\frac{1}{2}$) of each shape.

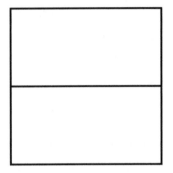  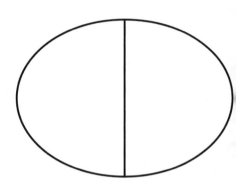

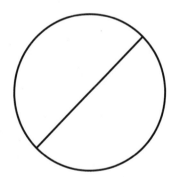 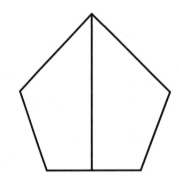 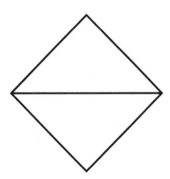

Do More: Cut circles, squares, triangles, and rectangles from colored paper. Fold them in half. What shape is half of a square? Is there more than one way to cut a square in half? Can you cut a square in half so that you end up with 2 triangles?

0-7424-1811-1 *Number & Operation*

Name _____ Date _____

One Fourth

$\frac{1}{4}$ One bat is shaded.
Four bats in all.

One fourth of the bats are shaded.

Directions: Color **one fourth** ($\frac{1}{4}$) of the balls in each group.

1.

2.

3.

4.

Do More: Draw a picture of 4 objects. Trade with a friend. Color one fourth of the objects.

McGraw-Hill Children's Publishing

0-7424-1811-1 *Number & Operations*

Name _____ Date _____

One Third

$\dfrac{1}{3}$ One book is colored.
Three books in all.

One third of the books are colored.

Directions: Does the picture show **one third** ($\dfrac{1}{3}$)? Circle yes or no.

Check your work. Pictures that show $\dfrac{1}{3}$ will have 1 part colored, 3 parts in all.

1.   **yes**   **no**

2.   **yes**   **no**

3.   **yes**   **no**

4.   **yes**   **no**

Do More: Count out 6 objects. Divide them in half. How many in each pile? Put them back in one pile again. Now divide the 6 objects into 3 equal groups. Which is more—one third or one half?

0-7424-1811-1 *Number & Operation*

Name _____ Date _____

Fraction Matching

$\frac{1}{5}$ One carrot is colored.
Five carrots in all.

One fifth of the carrots are colored.

Directions: Match each picture to its fraction. Write the fraction's name on the line. The first one has been done for you.

1.  $\frac{1}{6}$ _____

2.  $\frac{1}{4}$ _____

3. 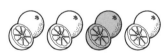 $\frac{1}{2}$ <u>one half</u>

4.  $\frac{1}{3}$ _____

Do More: Draw a picture of a lunch. How would you share it with a friend? Color your part red. Color your friend's part blue. Each of you gets **one half** of the lunch. Plan a lunch day and trade real lunches!

49

McGraw-Hill Children's Publishing   0-7424-1811-1 *Number & Operations*

Fractions of a Set

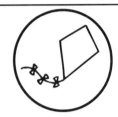 

$\frac{1}{3}$ One kite is circled.
Three kites in all.

One third of the kites are circled.

Directions: Circle the number of objects shown by the fraction.

1. $\frac{1}{4}$

2. $\frac{1}{2}$

3. $\frac{1}{3}$

4. $\frac{1}{2}$

Think: How would you show $\frac{2}{3}$? Draw a picture. Using your picture, explain to a friend how you solved the problem.

0-7424-1811-1 *Number & Operation*

Skills Checklist—Number Systems

❏ 1. Recognizes numerals 0–12.

❏ 2. Understands quantities 0–12.

❏ 3. Can read the number words 1–12.

❏ 4. Recognizes numerals 13–20.

❏ 5. Recognizes numerals 21–50.

❏ 6. Recognizes numerals 50–100.

❏ 7. Can count to 100.

❏ 8. Recognizes even numbers.

❏ 9. Recognizes odd numbers.

❏ 10. Can count by 2s to 20.

❏ 11. Can count by 5s to 50.

❏ 12. Can count by 10s to 100.

❏ 13. Understands base-ten and place value.

❏ 14. Recognizes multiple representations of the same number
         (base-ten, numeral, number word).

❏ 15. Recognizes "how many" in sets of objects.

❏ 16. Understands ordinals first through tenth.

❏ 17. Recognizes fractions $\frac{1}{2}$, $\frac{1}{4}$, and $\frac{1}{3}$.

❏ 18. Understands greater than >.

❏ 19. Understands less than <.

❏ 20. Understands equal numbers.

✗ = Needs continued work.
✓ = Has demonstrated comprehension.

51

Name _____ Date _____

Grouping

Directions: Gary collects stamps. He is sorting letters for his collection. Cut out the picture at the bottom of the page that shows how many letters and stamps. Count the total stamps. Solve the problem.

1. There are 3 letters.
There are 2 stamps on each letter.
How many stamps in all? _____

2. There are 2 letters.
There is 1 stamp on each letter.
How many stamps in all? _____

3. There are 2 letters.
There are 2 stamps on each letter.
How many stamps in all? _____

4. There is 1 letter.
There are 3 stamps on that letter.
How many stamps in all? _____

Cut out boxes →

0-7424-1811-1 *Number & Operation*

Name _____ Date _____

Grouping

Directions: Emma is cleaning the school library. She is putting books back on the shelves. Answer the questions about each bookshelf.

1.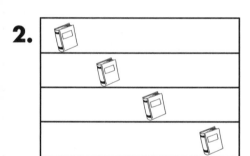

How many shelves? _____

How many books per shelf? _____

How many books in all? _____

2.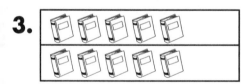

How many shelves? _____

How many books per shelf? _____

How many books in all? _____

3.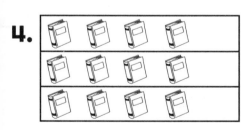

How many shelves? _____

How many books per shelf? _____

How many books in all? _____

4.

How many shelves? _____

How many books per shelf? _____

How many books in all? _____

Do More: For each problem on this page, write a problem that shows how many books. Share your problem with a friend and tell how you solved it.

McGraw-Hill Children's Publishing

0-7424-1811-1 *Number & Operations*

Name _____ Date _____

Sharing

Katie
red

Jared
blue

David
green

Su-Yi
purple

Peter
orange

Directions: Five friends are having a picnic lunch. Use the picture to color each friend's share of the food. Divide all the food equally between the 5 friends.

1.

2.

3.

4.

Do More: Each group of objects was shared by 5 friends. Write a division equation to show each problem. Example: For problem 1, 10 watermelon slices divided by 5 friends, or 10 ÷ 5.

More or Less?

2 + 3 = 5	5 − 3 = 2
When you **add,** you get **more.**	When you **subtract,** you get **less.**

Directions: For each problem, circle the first number. Then circle the answer. Is the answer more or less than the first number? If it is more, color in the ✚. If there is less, color in the ▭.

1.   7 ✚ 5 = 2

2.   4 ✚ 4 = 8

3.   8 ✚ 3 = 5

4.   10 ✚ 1 = 11

5.   5 ✚ 2 = 3

6.   12 ✚ 6 = 6

Do More: Use objects to prove the problems on this page. Example: For problem 1, count out 7 objects. Take away 5 objects. How many are left?

McGraw-Hill Children's Publishing

0-7424-1811-1 *Number & Operations*

Legs and Wings

Directions: Look at the animals for each problem. Write and solve each problem. The first two have been done for you.

1. How many legs on a  and a  ?

$4 + 4 = $ _____

2. How many wings on a  and a  ?

$2 + 0 = $ _____

3. How many more legs does a  have than a  ?

4. How many more legs does a  have than a  ?

Do More: Explain to a friend how you solved the problems. Did you use the pictures? What numbers did you need to use? How did you know?

0-7424-1811-1 *Number & Operation*

Name _____   Date _____

Sum and Difference

$$
\begin{array}{r} 3 \\ +\ 2 \\ \hline 5 \end{array}
$$
5 is the
sum.

When you add numbers,
you find the **sum**.

$$
\begin{array}{r} 5 \\ -\ 2 \\ \hline 3 \end{array}
$$
3 is the
difference.

When you subtract numbers,
you find the **difference**.

Directions: Solve the problems inside the bee. If you found a sum (**+**), color the space **yellow**. If you found a difference (**−**), color the space **black**.

$$
\begin{array}{r} 5 \\ +\ 2 \\ \hline \end{array}
$$

$$
\begin{array}{r} 6 \\ +\ 6 \\ \hline \end{array}
$$

$$
\begin{array}{r} 8 \\ +\ 2 \\ \hline \end{array}
$$

$$
\begin{array}{r} 7 \\ -\ 3 \\ \hline \end{array}
$$

$$
\begin{array}{r} 5 \\ +\ 6 \\ \hline \end{array}
$$

$$
\begin{array}{r} 4 \\ -\ 3 \\ \hline \end{array}
$$

$$
\begin{array}{r} 9 \\ +\ 1 \\ \hline \end{array}
$$

$$
\begin{array}{r} 10 \\ -\ 5 \\ \hline \end{array}
$$

McGraw-Hill Children's Publishing

0-7424-1811-1 *Number & Operations*

Name _____ Date _____

Eight, Nine, or Ten?

Directions: Solve the problems at the bottom of the page. Cut the problems apart. Then glue each one in the box with the right answer.

8	9	10

7 + 2 = _____	5 + 5 = _____	11 − 3 = _____
4 + 6 = _____	5 + 3 = _____	10 − 1 = _____
12 − 2 = _____	5 + 4 = _____	6 + 3 = _____

0-7424-1811-1 *Number & Operatio*

Name _____ Date _____

Adding Back and Forth

Directions: Solve the problems. Draw a line from the engine to the freight car with the same answer.

$8 + 7 =$ _____

$1 + 5 =$ _____

$3 + 6 =$ _____

$3 + 9 =$ _____

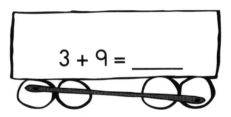
$5 + 1 =$ _____

$7 + 8 =$ _____

$9 + 3 =$ _____

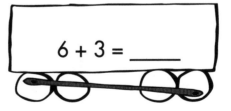
$6 + 3 =$ _____

Think: Does it matter what order you add numbers? Is $3 + 2$ the same as $2 + 3$?

McGraw-Hill Children's Publishing

0-7424-1811-1 *Number & Operations*

Name _____ Date _____

Trading Card Take-Away

Directions: Use the pictures to solve the problems. Draw the correct number of baseball cards to complete the problem.

1. Angela had 8 baseball cards.

She gave some to Josh.

—

Now Angela has 6 cards.

How many cards did she give to Josh?_____

2. D'Andre had 6 baseball

cards. He gave some cards to

Jason. Now D'Andre has 4 cards.

—

How many did he give to Jason?_____

3. Mary had 7 baseball cards.

She gave some to Rachel as a trade.

Now Mary has 1 card left.

—

How many did she give to Rachel?_____

Do More: Get a collection of objects. Count the objects with a friend. Your friend looks away while you take some away. Count again. Can your friend guess how many you took away?

0-7424-1811-1 *Number & Operation*

Name _____   Date _____

Proving the Facts – Addition

Directions: Look at the equations. Circle the right number of dots to prove
the equations are equal. The first one has been done for you.

1. 5 + 6 = ___ (● ● ● ● ● ●)(● ● ● ● ● ●)

 6 + 5 = ___ (● ● ● ● ● ●)(● ● ● ● ●)

2. 4 + 8 = ___   ● ● ● ● ● ● ● ● ● ● ● ●

 8 + 4 = ___   ● ● ● ● ● ● ● ● ● ● ● ●

3. 3 + 11 = ___   ● ● ● ● ● ● ● ● ● ● ● ● ● ●

 11 + 3 = ___   ● ● ● ● ● ● ● ● ● ● ● ● ● ●

4. 6 + 7 = ___   ● ● ● ● ● ● ● ● ● ● ● ● ●

 7 + 6 = ___   ● ● ● ● ● ● ● ● ● ● ● ● ●

Do More: Write your own addition problems with the same answer.
Trade with a friend. Use dots to prove the problems are equal. Explain
how you solved the problem using the dots.

McGraw-Hill Children's Publishing   0-7424-1811-1 *Number & Operations*

Name _____ Date _____

Proving the Facts–Subtraction

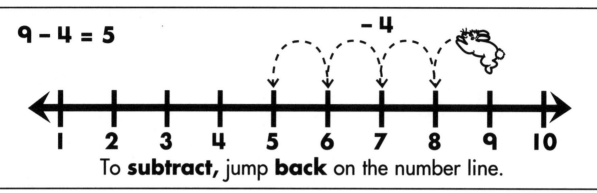

$9 - 4 = 5$

$- 4$

To **subtract**, jump **back** on the number line.

Directions: Solve the problems. Use the number line to prove your answer.

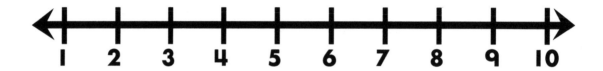

1. $9 - 3 =$ ____

2. $7 - 1 =$ ____

3. $5 - 5 =$ ____

4. $6 - 4 =$ ____

5. What problem does the number line show? Circle the right answer.

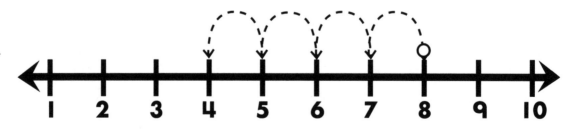

$8 - 2$ $10 - 4$ $10 - 8$ $8 - 4$

0-7424-1811-1 *Number & Operatio*

Name _____ Date _____

Proving the Facts

5 + 3 = 8 and 8 − 3 = 5 are **opposite problems.**
Both problems use the same numbers—**5**, **3**, and **8**.
The problems can be used to prove each other.

Directions: Solve the problems. Match each addition problem to its opposite subtraction problem.

1.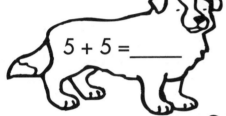
5 + 5 = _____

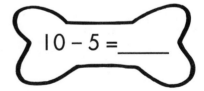
9 − 1 = _____

1.
5 + 5 = _____

2.
2 + 7 = _____

3.
7 + 4 = _____

4.
8 + 1 = _____

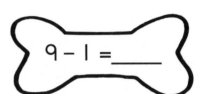
9 − 1 = _____

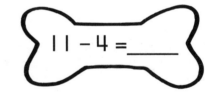
11 − 4 = _____

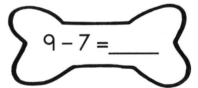
9 − 7 = _____

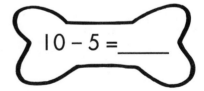
10 − 5 = _____

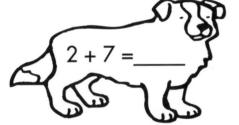
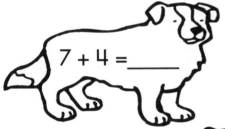
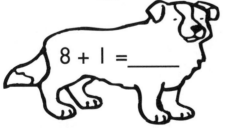

Think: There are 2 subtraction problems that could prove the addition problem 3 + 2 = 5. Can you name both?

McGraw-Hill Children's Publishing

0-7424-1811-1 *Number & Operations*

Name _____ Date _____

Take Two

$(3 + 2) + 7$ $3 + (2 + 7)$

$5 + 7 = 12$ $3 + 9 = 12$

To add 3 numbers together, start by adding any 2.

Directions: Solve the problems. Circle any 2 numbers. Add them together. Then add the third number.

1. $6 + 1 + 2 =$ _____   **2.** $5 + 4 + 1 =$ _____

3. $3 + 3 + 0 =$ _____   **4.** $2 + 2 + 8 =$ _____

5. $1 + 7 + 5 =$ _____   **6.** $9 + 1 + 4 =$ _____

Do More: Compare papers with a friend. Explain how you solved each problem. Does it matter which 2 numbers you circled first? Why or why not?

0-7424-1811-1 *Number & Operation*

Name _____   Date _____

Cookie Sale

Maria had 5 boxes of cookies. She sold 3 boxes.
How many does she have left?

$$5 - 3 = 2$$

Directions: The students at Orange Grove School sold cookies. Draw a picture and write a number problem for each question. Then solve the problem.

1. Kwan had 4 boxes of cookies. He sold 3 boxes. How many does he have left?

2. Eli had 7 boxes of cookies. He sold some. He has 4 boxes left. How many boxes did he sell?

3. Tara bought 2 boxes of cookies from Juan and 2 boxes from Lisa. How many does she have in all?

4. Isabelle had 4 boxes of cookies. She sold 2 boxes. How many does she have left?

Do More: Share your pictures and problems with a friend. Explain how you decided what to draw for each problem.

McGraw-Hill Children's Publishing   0-7424-1811-1 *Number & Operations*

Name _____ Date _____

Eleven or Twelve?

Directions: Add or subtract a number in each shape to make an equation equal to 11 or 12. The first one has been done for you.

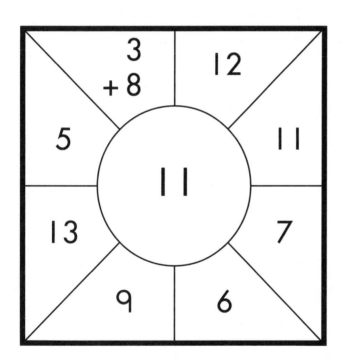

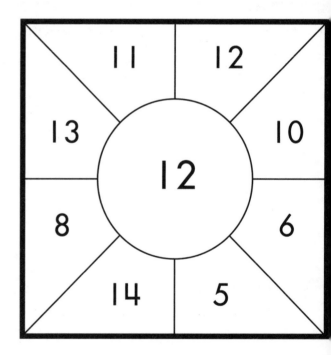

Do More: For each time you had to **add,** color the shape **orange**. For each time you had to **subtract,** color the shape **green**.

0-7424-1811-1 *Number & Operations*

Name _____ Date _____

No Change

$$5 \; + \; \boxed{4 \; - \; 4} \; = \; 5 \qquad\qquad 5 \; + \; 0 \; = \; 5$$

If you **add** and then **subtract** the same number, it is the same as adding 0.

Directions: Solve the following problems.

1. $10 + 1 - 1 =$ _____

$10 + 0 =$ _____

2. $3 + 3 - 3 =$ _____

$3 + 0 =$ _____

3. $5 + 2 - 2 =$ _____

$5 + 0 =$ _____

4. $2 + 6 - 6 =$ _____

$2 + 0 =$ _____

Think: Would the answers be the same if you subtracted and then added the same number? Is $5 - 4 + 4$ the same as $5 + 4 - 4$? Draw a picture to prove your answer.

McGraw-Hill Children's Publishing

0-7424-1811-1 *Number & Operations*

Name _____ Date _____

Mice and Cheese

Directions: Four mice went looking for cheese. Sometimes they found cheese and sometimes they dropped cheese. Follow each mouse's path. Add or subtract the amount of cheese. Write each mouse's total at the end of the path.

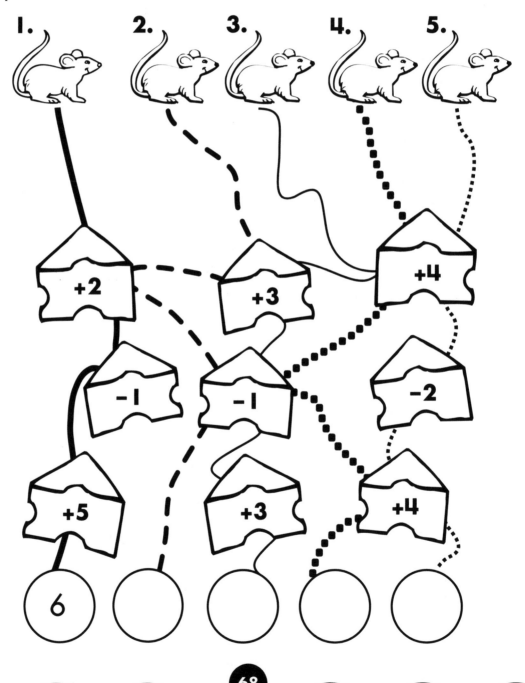

0-7424-1811-1 *Number & Operatio*

Name _____ Date _____

Missing Signs _____

Directions: To complete the equations, fill in the missing signs. One must be an addition problem and one must be a subtraction problem. The first one has been done for you.

1. 10 − 4 = 6

10 = 4 + 6

2. 12 ☐ 4 ☐ 8

12 ☐ 4 ☐ 8

3. 11 ☐ 3 ☐ 8

11 ☐ 3 ☐ 8

4. 10 ☐ 5 ☐ 5

10 ☐ 5 ☐ 5

5. 9 ☐ 4 ☐ 5

9 ☐ 4 ☐ 5

6. 7 ☐ 3 ☐ 4

7 ☐ 3 ☐ 4

Do More: Say each problem on this page using words. Example: ten minus four equals six; ten equals four plus six.

McGraw-Hill Children's Publishing

0-7424-1811-1 *Number & Operations*

Name _____ Date _____

Snail Race

Directions: Four snails are racing. Sometimes they get mixed up and crawl backwards for a while. Solve the equation for each snail's path. The first one has been done for you.

1.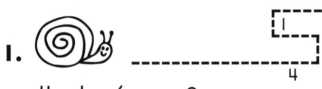

   $4 - 1 + 6 = \underline{\quad 9 \quad}$

2. $2 - 2 + 9 = \underline{\qquad}$

3. $5 - 3 + 7 = \underline{\qquad}$

4. $7 - 3 + 6 = \underline{\qquad}$

5. $3 - 3 + 10 = \underline{\qquad}$

70

0-7424-1811-1 *Number & Operations*

Name _____ Date _____

Count on Us

Directions: Solve the problems. Draw your answer as a picture and as a numeral.

1. 🐚🐚🐚 **+** 🐚🐚🐚 🐚🐚 = _____

2. ✒✒✒✒✒ **-** ✒✒✒ ✒✒✒✒✒ ✒✒✒ = _____

3. 🎈🎈🎈🎈 **+** 🎈🎈🎈 🎈🎈🎈 🎈🎈🎈 = _____

4. 🐛🐛🐛🐛 🐛🐛🐛🐛 **+** 🐛🐛🐛🐛 = _____

5. 🐱🐱🐱🐱 **-** 🐱🐱🐱 🐱🐱🐱 = _____

Do More: Write the numbers for each picture problem on this page.

McGraw-Hill Children's Publishing 0-7424-1811-1 *Number & Operations*

Name _____ Date _____

Climbing Calculation Mountain

Directions: Add or subtract the number pairs connected by a line. Place the sum or difference in the circle found at the top of the number pair. Work your way to the top of the mountain.

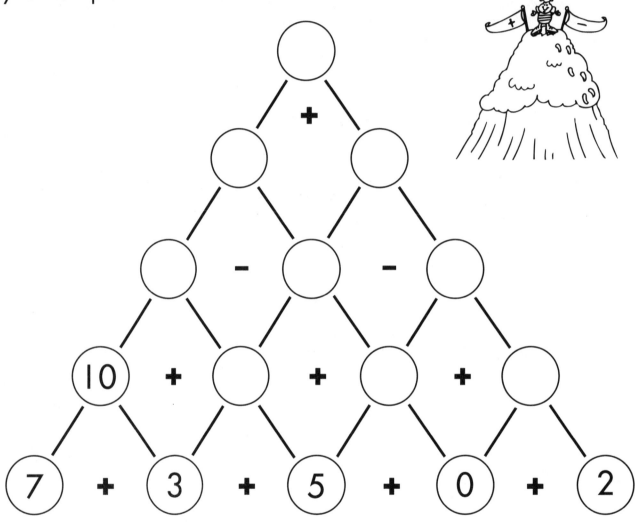

Do More: Build your own number "mountain." Start with 5 circles. Write in any number you want for each circle. Draw more circles for the rest of the "mountain." Trade puzzles with a friend and work them.

0-7424-1811-1 *Number & Operatio*

Name _____ Date _____

Frogs in a Well

Directions: Five frogs hopped out of an 8-foot well. Sometimes they fell backwards, but eventually they all made it out. Look at the equations. Draw each frog's path from the well. The first one has been done for you.

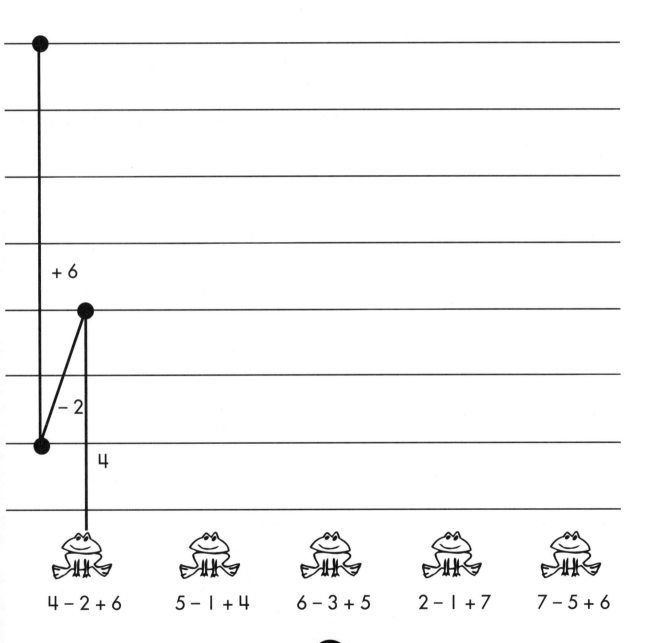

$+6$

-2

4

$4 - 2 + 6$ $5 - 1 + 4$ $6 - 3 + 5$ $2 - 1 + 7$ $7 - 5 + 6$

McGraw-Hill Children's Publishing

0-7424-1811-1 *Number & Operations*

Fact Families

$$3 + 4 = 7 \qquad 7 - 4 = 3$$
$$4 + 3 = 7 \qquad 7 - 3 = 4$$

You can use the same numbers in different ways.
These problems are all part of the same **fact family**.

Directions: Write 4 different problems for each group of numbers below.

1. 1, 2, 3

_____

_____

_____

_____

2. 5, 6, 11

_____

_____

_____

_____

3. 3, 9, 12

_____

_____

_____

_____

4. 4, 9, 13

_____

_____

_____

_____

0-7424-1811-1 *Number & Operatic*

Name _____ Date _____

Fact Families

$$10 + 11 = 21 \qquad 21 - 11 = 10$$
$$11 + 10 = 21 \qquad 21 - 10 = 11$$

You can use the same numbers in different ways.
These problems are all part of the same **fact family**.

Directions: Write 4 different problems for each group of numbers below.

1. 8, 9, 17

_____

_____

_____

_____

2. 20, 22, 42

_____

_____

_____

_____

3. 5, 11, 16

_____

_____

_____

_____

4. 4, 14, 18

_____

_____

_____

_____

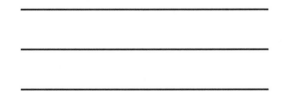
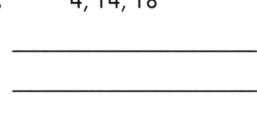

Think: Can a fact family have all even numbers? All odd? Try some problems to prove your answer.

McGraw-Hill Children's Publishing   0-7424-1811-1 *Number & Operations*

Name _____ Date _____

Equal Sets

Directions: First draw the needed items to make the sets equal.
Then answer the questions.

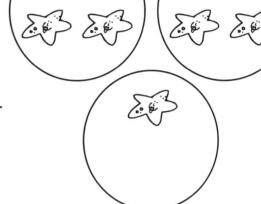

1. How many ◯s? _____

How many 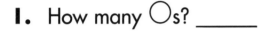 in each ◯? _____

How many ⭐ in all? _____

2. How many ☐s? _____

How many 🦀s in each ☐? _____

How many 🦀s in all? _____

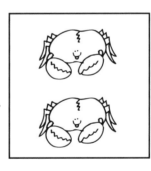

3. How many △s? _____

How many 🐟 in each △? _____

How many 🐟 in all? _____

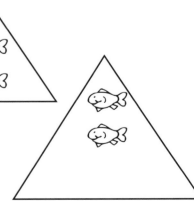

0-7424-1811-1 *Number & Operatio*

Name _____ Date _____

Repeated Addition

3 + 3 + 3 = 9   3 sets of 3 = 9

Directions: Use the pictures to solve the problems.

1. +

4 + 4 = _____

2 sets of 4 = _____

2.

2 + 2 + 2 + 2 = _____

4 sets of 2 = _____

3.

| + | + | + | + | + | + | + | = _____

_____ sets of _____ = _____

Think: What do you notice about the answers on this page? Can you think of 3 different ways to get the answer 6?

McGraw-Hill Children's Publishing   0-7424-1811-1 *Number & Operations*

Name _____ Date _____

Share the Snack

Directions: Four friends have been playing soccer. When the game is over, they have a snack. There are 12 fruit bars. How many will each friend have?

Color my fruit bars green.

Color my fruit bars blue.

Color my fruit bars orange.

Color my fruit bars yellow.

Do More: Share a snack. Get a group of 4 friends. Take out 2 graham crackers. Decide how to break the crackers so everyone gets the same amount. Eat your snack.

0-7424-1811-1 *Number & Operatio*

Skills Checklist–Operations

1. Understands the meaning of addition.

2. Understands the meaning of subtraction.

3. Chooses between addition or subtraction to show the relationship between a group of numbers.

4. Knows the meaning of the words **sum** and **difference**.

5. Understands the concept of commutativity. (2 + 3 = 3 + 2)

6. Understands the effect of adding whole numbers.

7. Understands the effect of subtracting whole numbers.

8. Uses pictures to solve addition problems.

9. Uses pictures to solve subtraction problems.

10. Can write number problems based on word and picture situations.

11. Can solve for a missing value when given quantity before and after.

12. Uses number line to solve problems.

13. Recognizes "opposite" problems (1 + 2 = 3 and 3 – 2 = 1).

14. Understands how addition and subtraction are related.

15. Understands associativity. (3 + 2) + 7 = 3 + (2 + 7).

16. Can solve problems involving both addition and subtraction.

17. Recognizes fractions $\frac{1}{2}$, $\frac{1}{4}$, $\frac{1}{3}$.

18. Understands that adding and subtracting the same number is the same as adding 0.

19. Understands fact families. (2 + 3 = 5, 3 + 2 = 5, 5 – 2 = 3, 5 – 3 = 2)

20. Knows how to make equal sets of objects.

21. Understands repeated sets of objects can be added.

22. Understands how to divide or share a quantity of items by making smaller groups.

= Needs continued work.

= Has demonstrated comprehension.

McGraw-Hill Children's Publishing

0-7424-1811-1 *Number & Operations*

Domino Addition

Directions: Count the dots on each domino. Solve each problem. Draw a line to connect problems with the same answer.

1. 6 + 1 = 7

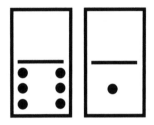

2. 4 + 4 = ____

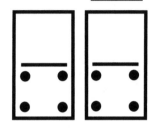

3. 2 + 6 = ____

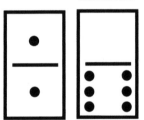

4. 5 + 4 = ____

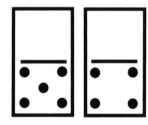

5. 3 + 6 = ____

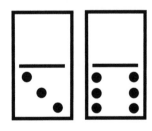

6. 5 + 2 = ____

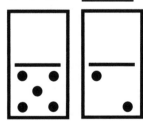

Do More: Does it matter what order you add numbers? Draw a picture to find out. Explain to a friend what you learned.

0-7424-1811-1 *Number & Operatic*

Name _____ Date _____

The Color Wheel

Directions: Color the wheel with 1 part red, 2 parts blue, and 3 parts yellow. Then use the wheel to write and solve the equations.

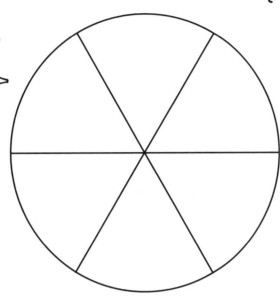

red = 1
blue = 2
yellow = 3

1. What is the total of the red part plus the blue parts?

1 + 2 = _____

2. What is the total of yellow parts plus blue parts?

_____ + _____ = _____

3. What is the total of the red part plus yellow parts?

_____ + _____ = _____

4. What is the total of the red, yellow, and blue parts?

_____ + _____ + _____ = _____

Do More: What fraction of the circle is red? What fraction is blue? What fraction is yellow?

McGraw-Hill Children's Publishing

0-7424-1811-1 *Number & Operations*

Name _____ Date _____

Eight and Its Pairs

Directions: Look at the pictures and write an equation. Then look at the equations and draw a picture for each one. Solve the problems.

1. ⚾ ⚾ ⚾ ⚾ + ⚾ ⚾ ⚾ ⚾ _____ $4 + 4 = 8$

2. 🏈 🏈 🏈 + 🏈 🏈 🏈 🏈 🏈 _____

3. ⚽ ⚽ ⚽ ⚽ ⚽ ⚽ + ⚽ ⚽ _____

4. $7 + 1 =$ ____

5. $2 + 6 =$ ____

6. $5 + 3 =$ ____

Do More: All together, there are 9 different number pairs with a sum of 8. Can you list them?

0-7424-1811-1 *Number & Operation*

Name _____ Date _____

Nifty Nine

Directions: Use the pictures to help you solve the equations.

1. $6 + 3 = 9$ +

2. $2 + 7 = $ _____   +

3. $1 + 8 = $ _____   +

4. $4 + 5 = $ _____   +

5. $5 + 4 = $ _____ 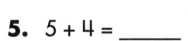 +

Think: Is $4 + 5$ the same as $5 + 4$? Draw a picture to prove yes or no.

McGraw-Hill Children's Publishing 0-7424-1811-1 *Number & Operations*

Name _____ Date _____

Totally Ten

Directions: Do you know the number pairs with a sum of 10? Draw sets of sticks, stones, or anything you choose to illustrate and prove each equation. The first one has been done for you.

1.   6   +   4   =   10

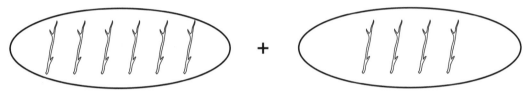

2.   3   +   7   = _____

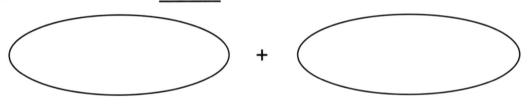

3.   2   +   8   = _____

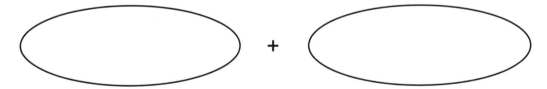

4.   5   +   5   = _____

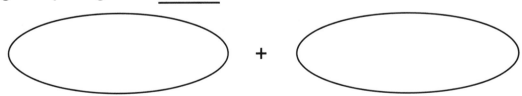

Think: How many different ways can you add 2 numbers together to make 10?

0-7424-1811-1 *Number & Operations*

Name _____ Date _____

Flying Sums

Directions: Solve the problems. Then use the code to color the design.

yellow = 8
red = 9
blue = 10

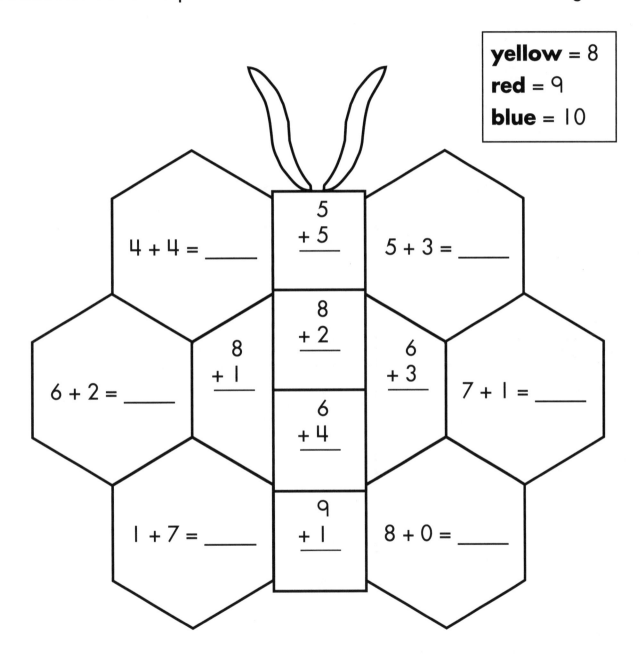

$4 + 4 =$ ____

$\begin{array}{r} 5 \\ + 5 \\ \hline \end{array}$

$5 + 3 =$ ____

$6 + 2 =$ ____

$\begin{array}{r} 8 \\ + 1 \\ \hline \end{array}$

$\begin{array}{r} 8 \\ + 2 \\ \hline \end{array}$

$\begin{array}{r} 6 \\ + 4 \\ \hline \end{array}$

$\begin{array}{r} 6 \\ + 3 \\ \hline \end{array}$

$7 + 1 =$ ____

$1 + 7 =$ ____

$\begin{array}{r} 9 \\ + 1 \\ \hline \end{array}$

$8 + 0 =$ ____

Do More: Use pattern blocks to match the pieces for each problem.

McGraw-Hill Children's Publishing

0-7424-1811-1 *Number & Operations*

Name _____ Date _____

Totaling Towers

Directions: Which tower will be the tallest? Look at the problems at the bottom of the page to make your guess. Then solve the problems by coloring in the towers. Did you guess right?

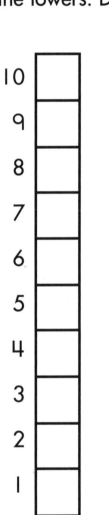

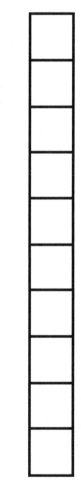

10					10
9					9
8					8
7					7
6					6
5					5
4					4
3					3
2					2
1					1

$$\begin{array}{r} 4 \\ +4 \\ \hline \end{array} \qquad \begin{array}{r} 3 \\ +7 \\ \hline \end{array} \qquad \begin{array}{r} 5 \\ +4 \\ \hline \end{array} \qquad \begin{array}{r} 6 \\ +1 \\ \hline \end{array} \qquad \begin{array}{r} 7 \\ +2 \\ \hline \end{array}$$

0-7424-1811-1 *Number & Operatio*

Name _____ Date _____

Tiptoe through the Tulips

Directions: Use the tulips to practice addition facts. Cover 1 number with your finger. Find the sum of the other 2 numbers. Repeat, covering a different number each time.

Do More: Write 3 different addition problems for each tulip on this page. Quiz a friend. See if you can answer the problems without writing anything down.

McGraw-Hill Children's Publishing

0-7424-1811-1 *Number & Operations*

Name _____ Date _____

Finding the Sum of Three Numbers

Directions: Circle the 2 numbers in each problem with a sum of 10. Then add the last number. The first one has been done for you.

1. (3 + 7) + 3 = _____

  10 + 3 = 13

2. 1 + 9 + 3 = _____

3. 4 + 8 + 2 = _____

4. 7 + 3 + 6 = _____

5. 6 + 7 + 4 = _____

6. 2 + 8 + 9 = _____

Do More: Compare papers with a friend. Explain how you solved each problem. Can you find a different way to solve these problems?

0-7424-1811-1 *Number & Operation*

Adding with Cubes

Directions: Find the sums. Then draw a line to the picture that proves the answer. Circle all the groups of 10 in each picture. The first one has been done for you.

1. $38 + 5 =$ _____   **a.**

2. $20 + 6 =$ _____   **b.**

3. $14 + 4 =$ _____   **c.**

4. $11 + 9 =$ _____   **d.**

5. $15 + 1 =$ _____   **e.**

Do More: Use your own base-ten cubes to show the problems on this page.

McGraw-Hill Children's Publishing

0-7424-1811-1 *Number & Operations*

Name _____ Date _____

Adding with Regrouping

When you add, you may need to **regroup** the ones and tens.

Add the ones first.
8 + 4 = 12

Regroup.
12 = 1 ten and 2 ones

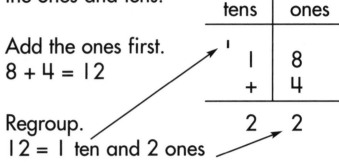

tens	ones
1	8
+	4
2	2

Directions: Solve the following problems. Regroup the tens and ones.

1.

tens	ones
1	9
+	4

2.

tens	ones
1	4
+	8

3.

tens	ones
2	5
+	9

4.

tens	ones
1	8
+	7

0-7424-1811-1 *Number & Operatio*

Name _____ Date _____

Adding Your Way

The same problem can be solved more than one way.

$25 + 7 = 32$

	tens	ones	
Regroup → Regroup 1 ten.	{ 1		
	2	5 }	$5 + 7 = 12$
	+	7 }	
	3	2	$12 = 1$ ten 2 ones

You can draw a **picture**.   You can **regroup** the tens and ones.

Directions: Solve the problems any way you can. Once you have the answers, explain to a friend how you got them. Did you draw a picture? Did you regroup? Did you do something else?

1. $17 + 7 =$ _____

2. $38 + 7 =$ _____

3. $27 + 5 =$ _____

4. $11 + 9 =$ _____

5. $23 + 8 =$ _____

6. $15 + 6 =$ _____

Do More: Go back over the problems on this page. Solve them a different way.

McGraw-Hill Children's Publishing   0-7424-1811-1 *Number & Operations*

Name _____ Date _____

Subtracting Is Hopping Backwards

Directions: Subtracting is counting backwards. The frog is hopping backwards. To solve the subtraction problems, draw the frog's path. The first one has been done for you.

1.

1   2   3   4   5   6   7   8   9   10 $5 - 2 = 3$

2.

1   2   3   4   5   6   7   8   9   10 $6 - 4 =$ _____

3.

1   2   3   4   5   6   7   8   9   10 $9 - 5 =$ _____

4.

1   2   3   4   5   6   7   8   9   10 $7 - 1 =$ _____

5.

1   2   3   4   5   6   7   8   9   10 $10 - 3 =$ _____

0-7424-1811-1 *Number & Operati*

Name _____ Date _____

Take Away in the Garden

Directions: Solve each problem by crossing out the number taken away. The first one has been done for you.

1. 5 – 2 = 3

2. 4 – 1 = _____

3. 6 – 3 = _____

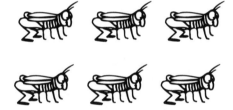

4. 8 – 4 = _____

5. 7 – 5 = _____

6. 9 – 3 = _____

Do More: Draw a picture with a certain number of objects crossed out. See if a friend can guess what number problem you have drawn.

McGraw-Hill Children's Publishing

0-7424-1811-1 *Number & Operations*

Name _____ Date _____

Domino Subtraction

Directions: Use the dominoes to help you solve each problem.

1. 5 – 1 = 4

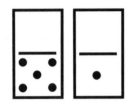

2. 3 – 2 = _____

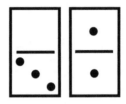

3. 4 – 1 = _____

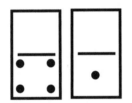

4. 5 – 2 = _____

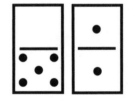

5. 6 – 4 = _____

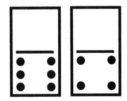

6. 4 – 3 = _____

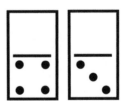

Do More: Draw a set of dominoes. Write the number problems each domino shows. Solve the problems.

0-7424-1811-1 *Number & Operation*

Name _____ Date _____

What's the Difference?

Directions: Find the difference. Then draw a line to connect each equation with its matching picture.

$- 1 =$ _____

$- 4 =$ _____

$- 4 =$ _____

$- 2 =$ _____

$- 5 =$ _____

$- 3 =$ _____

McGraw-Hill Children's Publishing

0-7424-1811-1 *Number & Operations*

Name _____ Date _____

Ten Bears in the Bed

Directions: Use the picture to solve the problems. Write a number sentence to match the problem.

1. There were 10 bears in a bed, and the little one said, "Roll over; I'm crowded." So they all rolled over, and 1 bear fell out. How many are left?

_____10_____ – _____1_____ = _____

2. There were 8 bears in a bed, and the little one said, "Roll over; I'm crowded." So they all rolled over, and this time 2 bears fell out. How many are left?

_____ – _____ = _____

3. When there were 7 bears in a bed, the little one said, "Roll over; I'm crowded." So they all rolled over, and this time 3 bears fell out. How many are left?

_____ – _____ = _____

4. When there were 3 bears in a bed, the little one said, "Roll over; I'm crowded." So they all rolled over, and kept rolling, and this time all 3 fell out! How many are left?

_____ – _____ = _____

0-7424-1811-1 *Number & Operatio*

Name _____ Date _____

Difference of One or Two

irections: Write a number in the box to make a difference of 1 or 2.

1. $1 - \boxed{} = 1$

2. $2 - \boxed{} = 2$

3. $6 - \boxed{} = 1$

4. $5 - \boxed{} = 2$

5. $7 - \boxed{} = 1$

6. $8 - \boxed{} = 2$

o More: Make your own number problem with a missing number. ade papers with a friend. Solve the problems.

McGraw-Hill Children's Publishing

0-7424-1811-1 *Number & Operations*

Name _____ Date _____

Prove It

Directions: Find the difference. Cross out the bubbles being taken away. Then count the bubbles that are left to prove your answer.

1. $10 - 5 =$ _____

○ ○ ○ ○ ○
○ ○ ○ ○ ○

2. $8 - 3 =$ _____

○ ○ ○ ○
○ ○ ○ ○

3. $7 - 6 =$ _____

○ ○ ○
○ ○ ○

4. $5 - 1 =$ _____

○ ○ ○ ○ ○

5. $9 - 6 =$ _____

○ ○ ○ ○
○ ○ ○ ○ ○

6. $6 - 4 =$ _____

○ ○ ○
○ ○ ○

Do More: Draw a picture with some bubbles crossed out. Then write the number problem for the picture.

0-7424-1811-1 *Number & Operati*

Name _____ Date _____

Coloring Differences

Directions: Solve the problems. Then use the code to color the design.

yellow = 5
red = 6
blue = 7

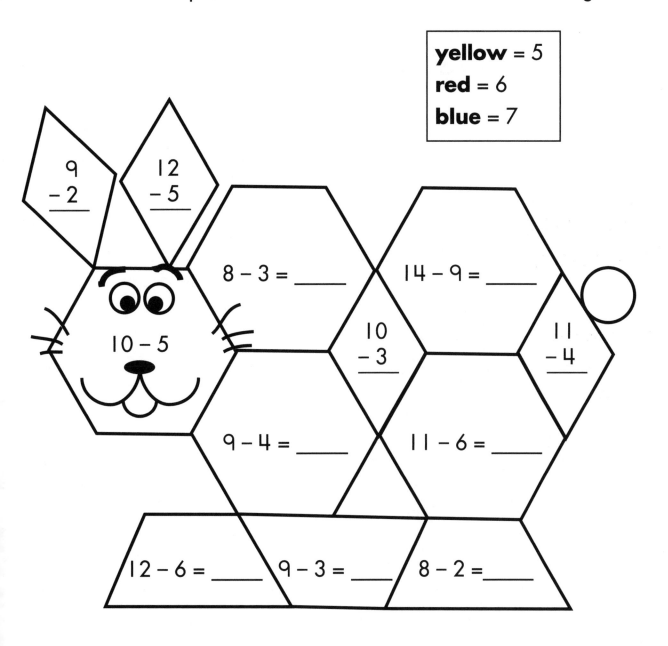

$\begin{array}{r} 9 \\ -2 \\ \hline \end{array}$

$\begin{array}{r} 12 \\ -5 \\ \hline \end{array}$

$8 - 3 =$ ____

$14 - 9 =$ ____

$10 - 5$

$\begin{array}{r} 10 \\ -3 \\ \hline \end{array}$

$\begin{array}{r} 11 \\ -4 \\ \hline \end{array}$

$9 - 4 =$ ____

$11 - 6 =$ ____

$12 - 6 =$ ____ $9 - 3 =$ ____ $8 - 2 =$ ____

Do More: Use pattern blocks to match the pieces for each problem.

McGraw-Hill Children's Publishing

0-7424-1811-1 *Number & Operations*

Name _____ Date _____

Number Bars

Directions: Use the number bars to find the missing number.

1. 12 – ☐ = 6

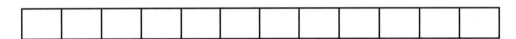

2. 10 – ☐ = 3

3. 8 – ☐ = 2

4. 11 – ☐ = 5

5. 15 – ☐ = 1

Think: How did you use the number bars to solve the problems?
Compare ideas with a friend.

0-7424-1811-1 *Number & Operatio*

Name _____ Date _____

Tumble-Down Tower

irections: Use the tower to write and solve equations. The tower has
2 blocks in all.

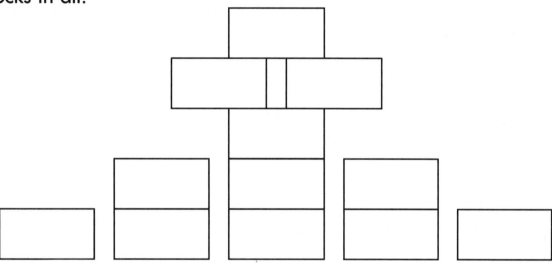

1. If the top block on the tower is taken away, how many blocks are left?

$$\underline{\quad 12 \quad} - \underline{\quad 1 \quad} = \underline{\qquad}$$

2. If the blocks on the top 2 rows are taken away, how many blocks are left?

$$\underline{\qquad} - \underline{\qquad} = \underline{\qquad}$$

3. If the blocks on the top 4 rows are taken away, how many blocks are left?

$$\underline{\qquad} - \underline{\qquad} = \underline{\qquad}$$

4. If the blocks on the top 3 rows are taken away, how many blocks are left?

$$\underline{\qquad} - \underline{\qquad} = \underline{\qquad}$$

o More: Build a tower with 12 blocks. How many different ways can
ou use the 12 blocks to make a 5-level tower?

cGraw-Hill Children's Publishing   0-7424-1811-1 *Number & Operations*

Name _____ Date _____

Subtracting with Regrouping

When you add, you may need to **regroup** the ones and tens.

Regroup.

22 = 1 ten and
         12 ones

tens	ones
$\cancel{2}^{1}$	$^{1}2$
−	4
1	8

Directions: Solve the following problems. Regroup the tens and ones.

1.

tens	ones
4	0
−	1

2.

tens	ones
2	4
−	8

3.

tens	ones
3	5
−	6

4.

tens	ones
1	8
−	9

0-7424-1811-1 *Number & Operati*

Subtracting Your Way

The same problem can be solved more than one way.

32 – 7 = 25

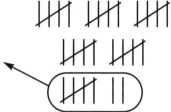

tens	ones
$\overset{2}{\cancel{3}}$	$\overset{1}{2}$
–	7
2	5

You can draw a **picture.**　　　You can **regroup** the tens and ones.

Directions: Solve the problems any way you can. Once you have the answers, explain to a friend how you got them. Did you draw a picture? Did you regroup? Did you do something else?

1. 18 – 9 = _____

2. 37 – 5 = _____

3. 25 – 1 = _____

4. 11 – 4 = _____

5. 21 – 2 = _____

6. 36 – 7 = _____

Do More: Go back over the problems on this page. Solve them a different way.

McGraw-Hill Children's Publishing　　　0-7424-1811-1 *Number & Operations*

Name _____ Date _____

Pot of Gold

Directions: There are 12 coins inside the pot of gold. Use the coins to solv
the word problems.

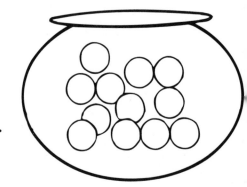

1. Jen takes away 5 coins.

How many are left? _____

2. Michael reaches in and takes 7 coins.

How many are left? _____

3. Maria adds 3 coins to the pot.

How many are there now? _____

4. Chantel takes away 2 coins.

How many are left? _____

5. Jordan, Samuel, and Rebecca each add 1 coin.

How many are there now? _____

6. The 9 members of the club take 1 coin each.

How many are left? _____

Do More: Draw a picture or write a number problem to show how
you got your answers.

Name _____ Date _____

The Fruit Bowl

rections: Use the code to draw and color fruits in the bowl. Then
ve the problems.

Draw	
1	banana
3	oranges
4	apples
5	plums

1. How many bananas and apples are in the bowl? _____

2. How many plums and oranges are in the bowl? _____

3. How many apples and oranges are in the bowl? _____

4. How many pieces of fruit are in the bowl all together? _____

McGraw-Hill Children's Publishing

0-7424-1811-1 *Number & Operations*

Name _____ Date _____

Guess

If you know that 5 + 5 = 10, you can
guess what 4 + 5 is. Since 4 + 5 is 1 less
than 5 + 5, guess that 4 + 5 is
1 less than 10, or 9.

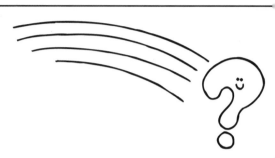

Directions: Don't count to find the sums. Begin by checking for pairs that
total 10. Use those numbers to guess other problems. When you are finished
guessing, solve the problems to check your guesses.

1. 2 + 8 = _____

    guess _____ answer _____

2. 2 + 7 = _____

    guess _____ answer _____

3. 5 + 5 = _____

    guess _____ answer _____

4. 7 + 5 = _____

    guess _____ answer _____

5. 4 + 6 = _____

    guess _____ answer _____

6. 4 + 9 = _____

    guess _____ answer _____

Do More: Explain to a friend how you made your guesses.

0-7424-1811-1 *Number & Operati*

Domino Problems

irections: Use the dominoes to help you solve each problem.

1. $2 + 4 = 6$

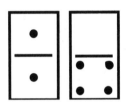

2. $10 - 5 =$ _____

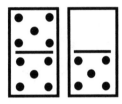

3. $4 + 4 =$ _____

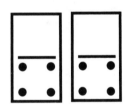

4. $12 - 6 =$ _____

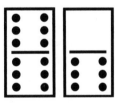

5. $5 + 1 =$ _____

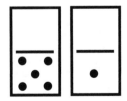

6. $8 - 4 =$ _____

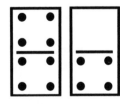

o More: Can you match each addition problem to a subtraction problem at proves its answer?

McGraw-Hill Children's Publishing

0-7424-1811-1 *Number & Operations*

Write the Problems

Directions: Write a problem for each picture. Then solve.

1.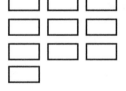

$$\underline{\qquad 9 - 2 = \qquad}$$

2. ○ ○ + ○ ○ ○
○ ○
○ ○
○ ○

_____

3. ☐ ☐ ☐ + ☐ ☐
☐ ☐ ☐
☐ ☐ ☐
☐ ☐ ☐
☐

_____

4.

_____

5.

_____

6.

_____

Name _____ Date _____

Two-Digit Addition and Subtraction Practice

rections: Solve the problems.

1. 23
     + 17

2. 16
     − 10

3. 43
     − 11

4. 52
     − 41

5. 30
     + 14

6. 21
     + 18

7. 19
     − 10

8. 40
     − 20

9. 33
     + 16

o More: Explain to a friend how you solved each problem. Did you aw a picture? Regroup tens and ones? Do something else?

cGraw-Hill Children's Publishing   0-7424-1811-1 *Number & Operations*

Name _____ Date _____

Estimating Candy

Directions: Guess how many candies are in each jar just by looking at it. Then use the candy to solve the problem.

1.

guess _____

$5 + 4 =$ _____

2.

guess _____

$5 + 5 + 3 =$ _____

3.

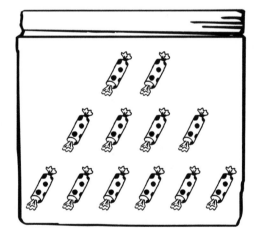

guess _____

$6 + 4 + 2 =$ _____

4.

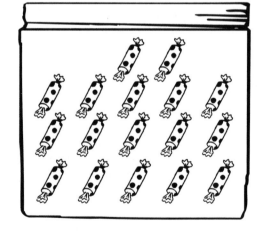

guess _____

$5 + 5 + 5 + 2 =$ _____

Think: Did estimating help you solve the problem?

110

0-7424-1811-1 *Number & Operat*

Name _____ Date _____

Don't Count the Stars

Directions: Don't count the stars. Guess how many in each set by rounding off to the nearest 10. Then prove your guess by solving the problem.

1. ☆ ☆ ☆ ☆ ☆ ☆ ☆ ☆ ☆ ☆
☆ ☆ ☆ ☆ ☆ ☆ ☆ ☆ ☆ ☆
☆ ☆

rounded off to nearest ten = _____
20 + 2 = _____

2. ☆ ☆ ☆ ☆ ☆ ☆ ☆ ☆ ☆ ☆
☆ ☆ ☆ ☆ ☆ ☆ ☆ ☆ ☆ ☆
☆ ☆ ☆ ☆ ☆ ☆ ☆ ☆

rounded off to nearest ten = _____
30 – 2 = _____

3. ☆ ☆ ☆ ☆ ☆ ☆ ☆ ☆ ☆ ☆
☆ ☆ ☆ ☆ ☆ ☆ ☆ ☆ ☆ ☆
☆ ☆ ☆ ☆ ☆ ☆ ☆ ☆ ☆ ☆
☆ ☆ ☆ ☆ ☆ ☆

rounded off to nearest ten = _____
40 – 4 = _____

4. ☆ ☆ ☆ ☆ ☆ ☆ ☆ ☆ ☆ ☆
☆ ☆ ☆ ☆ ☆ ☆ ☆ ☆ ☆ ☆
☆ ☆ ☆ ☆

rounded off to nearest ten = _____
20 + 4 = _____

5. ☆ ☆ ☆ ☆ ☆ ☆ ☆ ☆ ☆ ☆
☆ ☆ ☆ ☆ ☆ ☆ ☆ ☆ ☆ ☆
☆ ☆ ☆ ☆ ☆ ☆ ☆ ☆ ☆ ☆
☆ ☆ ☆ ☆

rounded off to nearest ten = _____
30 + 4 = _____

6. ☆ ☆ ☆ ☆ ☆ ☆ ☆ ☆ ☆ ☆
☆ ☆ ☆ ☆ ☆ ☆ ☆ ☆ ☆ ☆
☆ ☆ ☆ ☆ ☆ ☆ ☆ ☆ ☆ ☆
☆ ☆ ☆ ☆ ☆ ☆ ☆ ☆ ☆ ☆
☆ ☆ ☆ ☆ ☆ ☆ ☆ ☆ ☆

rounded off to nearest ten = _____
50 – 1 = _____

111

0-7424-1811-1 *Number & Operations*

Name _____ Date _____

Educated Guesses

Directions: Take a guess if the answer will be more or less. Then write 2 number problems to test your answer. The first one has been done for you.

1. Is 3 + 5 more or less than 10?   more   (less)

$3 + 5 = 8$ $8 < 10$

2. Is 6 + 5 more or less than 10?   more   less

_____

3. Is 7 + 4 more or less than 10?   more   less

_____

4. Is 5 + 2 more or less than 10?   more   less

_____

5. Is 6 + 6 more or less than 10?   more   less

_____

6. Is 3 + 4 more or less than 10?   more   less

_____

112

0-7424-1811-1 *Number & Operati*

Name _____ Date _____

Guess the Sums

rections: Before you solve the problems, guess the sum. Count the
mber of tens to help you guess. Circle your guess. To prove your work,
lve each equation.

1.
$$\begin{array}{r} 20 \\ + 21 \\ \hline \end{array}$$
49 39 41

2.
$$\begin{array}{r} 11 \\ + 30 \\ \hline \end{array}$$
59 41 39

3.
$$\begin{array}{r} 29 \\ + 10 \\ \hline \end{array}$$
39 70 49

4.
$$\begin{array}{r} 50 \\ + 11 \\ \hline \end{array}$$
41 61 71

5.
$$\begin{array}{r} 30 \\ + 19 \\ \hline \end{array}$$
49 59 69

ink: How else could you guess the answer to the problems on
s page?

cGraw-Hill Children's Publishing   0-7424-1811-1 *Number & Operations*

Name _____ Date _____

Solve It Your Way – Addition

Directions: Solve each problem your own way.

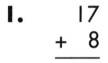

1. 17
    + 8

2. 20
    + 11

3. 33
    + 8

4. 14
    + 16

5. 27
    + 9

6. 39
    + 10

Do More: Draw the steps you took to solve the problem. Explain them to a friend.

0-7424-1811-1 *Number & Operati*

Name _____ Date _____

Solve It Your Way – Subtraction

rections: Solve each problem your own way.

1.
```
  34
- 10
____
```

2.
```
  42
- 12
____
```

3.
```
  19
- 17
____
```

4.
```
  28
-  8
____
```

5.
```
  37
-  9
____
```

6.
```
  15
-  6
____
```

o More: Draw the steps you took to solve the problem. Explain them to friend.

cGraw-Hill Children's Publishing

0-7424-1811-1 *Number & Operations*

Name _____ Date _____

Solve It Your Way

Directions: Solve each problem your own way.

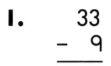

1. 33
    − 9
    _____

2. 19
    + 11
    _____

3. 16
    + 9
    _____

4. 20
    − 15
    _____

5. 38
    − 21
    _____

6. 22
    + 10
    _____

Do More: Draw the steps you took to solve the problem. Explain them to a friend.

0-7424-1811-1 *Number & Opera*

Skills Checklist—Computation

1. Uses estimation to solve addition problems.

2. Uses pictures to solve addition problems.

3. Uses objects to solve addition problems.

4. Uses mental computation to solve addition problems.

5. Proves addition answers using pictures.

6. Uses pictures to write addition problems.

7. Uses estimation to solve subtraction problems.

8. Uses pictures to solve subtraction problems.

9. Uses objects to solve subtraction problems.

10. Uses mental computation to solve subtraction problems.

11. Proves subtraction problems using pictures.

12. Uses pictures to write subtraction problems.

13. Understands how to regroup for addition problems.

14. Understands how to regroup for subtraction problems.

= Needs continued work.
= Has demonstrated comprehension.

McGraw-Hill Children's Publishing   0-7424-1811-1 *Number & Operations*

Answer Key

Pretest/Post Test 7–8
1. 2, 8, 18, 20
2. 9, 11, 15, 21
3. 18
4. 65
5. 80
6. 1, 45, 20, 98
7. 9, 32, 66
8. 0, 47, 96
9. Pictures will vary. Twenty-seven, fourteen.
10. <, >, =
11. Appropriate fraction should be colored in.
12. 18, 45
13. lion (circled), zebra (box around), snake (triangle around), cat (crossed out)
14. **a.** 4
    b. 7
    c. 7
15. **a.** 2
    b. 6
    c. 8
16. Answers will vary.

How Many? 10
4 snakes, 3 crabs, 5 starfish, 2 fish, 7 snails, 3 turtles, 1 camel (mystery animal)

Guess How Many 11
4 footballs, 7 soccer balls, 3 basketballs, 8 baseballs

Greater Than, Less Than (1–20) 16
1. >
2. <
3. >
4. <

Greater Than, Less Than (1–20) 17
1. <
2. <
3. >
4. <

Domino Totals 19
1. 21
2. 23
3. 22
4. 24
5. 25
6. 27

Sheep for Sale 23
1. $13
2. $23
3. $32
4. $43
5. $52

Lion's Share 24
1. 14
2. 32
3. 41
4. 11
5. 23

Greater Than, Less Than (21–50) 26
1. 33
2. 42
3. 27
4. 54
5. 40
6. 46

Greater Than, Less Than, or Equal? (21–50) 27
1. <
2. <
3. >
4. =
5. >
6. <

Counting by Tens 33
1. 3, 30¢
2. 7, 70¢
3. 4, 40¢
4. 8, 80¢
5. 6, 60¢

Number Patterns 36
1. 12, 14
2. 30, 35
3. 60, 70
4. 11, 13
5. 90, 100

Greater Than, Less Than, or Equal? (51–100) . . . . .
1. <
2. <
3. >
4. =
5. <
6. >

Greater Than, Less Than, or Equal? (51–100) . . . .
1. <
2. >
3. >
4. <
5. >
6. <

One Third . . . .
1. yes
2. no
3. yes
4. yes

Fraction Matching . . . . . .
1. $\frac{1}{2}$, one half
2. $\frac{1}{3}$, one third
3. $\frac{1}{4}$, one fourth
4. $\frac{1}{6}$, one sixth

Grouping . . . .
1. 6
2. 2
3. 4
4. 3

Grouping . . . .
1. 3, 2, 6
2. 4, 1, 4
3. 2, 5, 10
4. 3, 4, 12

Sharing . . . .
1. 2 slices each
2. 1 sandwich each
3. 3 cookies each
4. 1 juice box each

0-7424-1811-1 *Number & Operat*

Answer Key

3. $11 - 3 = 8$
   $11 = 3 + 8$
4. $10 - 5 = 5$
   $10 = 5 + 5$
5. $9 - 4 = 5$
   $9 = 4 + 5$
6. $7 - 3 = 4$
   $7 = 3 + 4$

1. $4 - 1 + 6 = 9$
2. $2 - 2 + 9 = 9$
3. $5 - 3 + 7 = 9$
4. $7 - 3 + 6 = 10$
5. $3 - 3 + 10 = 10$

1. $5 + 3 = 8$
2. $10 - 6 = 4$
3. $7 + 6 = 13$
4. $8 + 4 = 12$
5. $7 - 3 = 4$

1. $1 + 2 = 3, 2 + 1 = 3,$
   $3 - 1 = 2, 3 - 2 = 1$
2. $5 + 6 = 11, 6 + 5 = 11,$
   $11 - 5 = 6, 11 - 6 = 5$
3. $3 + 9 = 12, 9 + 3 = 12,$
   $12 - 3 = 9, 12 - 9 = 3$
4. $4 + 9 = 13, 9 + 4 = 13,$
   $13 - 4 = 9, 13 - 9 = 4$

1. $8 + 9 = 17, 9 + 8 = 17,$
   $17 - 8 = 9, 17 - 9 = 8$
2. $20 + 22 = 42, 22 + 20 = 42, 42 - 20 = 22,$
   $42 - 22 = 20$
3. $5 + 11 = 16, 11 + 5 = 16,$
   $16 - 11 = 5, 16 - 5 = 11$
4. $4 + 14 = 18, 14 + 4 = 18, 18 - 4 = 14,$
   $18 - 14 = 4$

1. $3, 3, 9$
2. $2, 2, 4$
3. $2, 5, 10$

1. $8, 8$
2. $8, 8$
3. $8, 8$ sets of $1 = 8$

1. $1 + 2 = 3$
2. $3 + 2 = 5$
3. $1 + 3 = 4$
4. $1 + 2 + 3 = 6$

1. 13
2. 13
3. 14
4. 16
5. 17
6. 19

1. $43, b$
2. $26, a$
3. $18, e$
4. $20, c$
5. $16, d$

1. 23
2. 22
3. 34
4. 25

cGraw-Hill Children's Publishing

0-7424-1811-1 *Number & Operations*

Answer Key

Adding Your Way 91
1. 24
2. 45
3. 32
4. 20
5. 31
6. 21

**Difference of One
or Two**. 97
1. 0
2. 0
3. 5
4. 3
5. 6
6. 6

Number Bars 100
1. 6
2. 7
3. 6
4. 6
5. 14

Tumble-Down Tower . . .101
1. $12 - 1 = 11$
2. $12 - 3 = 9$
3. $12 - 7 = 5$
4. $12 - 4 = 8$

**Subtracting with
Regrouping** 102
1. 39
2. 16
3. 29
4. 9

Subtracting Your Way .103
1. 9
2. 32
3. 24
4. 7
5. 19
6. 29

Pot of Gold 104
1. $12 - 5 = 7$
2. $12 - 7 = 5$
3. $12 + 3 = 15$
4. $12 - 2 = 10$
5. $12 + 3 = 15$
6. $12 - 9 = 3$

The Fruit Bowl 105
1. $1 + 4 = 5$
2. $5 + 3 = 8$
3. $4 + 3 = 7$
4. $1 + 3 + 4 + 5 = 13$

Guess 106
1. 10
2. 9
3. 10
4. 12
5. 10
6. 13

**Domino Problems—
Addition and
Subtraction** 107
1. 6
2. 5
3. 8
4. 6
5. 6
6. 4

Write the Problems 108
1. $9 - 2 = 7$
2. $8 + 3 = 11$
3. $13 + 2 = 15$
4. $12 - 4 = 8$
5. $13 - 6 = 7$
6. $11 + 7 = 18$

**Two-Digit Addition and
Subtraction Practice** . . . 109
1. 40
2. 6
3. 32
4. 11
5. 44
6. 39
7. 9
8. 20
9. 49

Estimating Candy 110
1. 9
2. 13
3. 12
4. 17

Don't Count the Stars . .111
1. 20, 22
2. 30, 28

3. 40, 36
4. 20, 24
5. 30, 34
6. 50, 49

Educated Guesses I
1. less, $3 + 5 = 8, 8 < 10$
2. more, $6 + 5 = 11, 11 >$
3. more, $7 + 4 = 11, 11 >$
4. less, $5 + 2 = 7, 7 < 10$
5. more, $6 + 6 = 12, 12 >$
6. less, $3 + 4 = 7, 7 < 10$

Guess the Sums I
1. 41
2. 41
3. 39
4. 61
5. 49

**Solve It Your Way—
Addition** I
1. 25
2. 31
3. 41
4. 30
5. 36
6. 49

**Solve It Your Way—
Subtraction** I
1. 24
2. 30
3. 2
4. 20
5. 28
6. 9

**Solve It Your Way—
Addition
and Subtraction** I
1. 24
2. 30
3. 25
4. 5
5. 17
6. 32

0-7424-1811-1 *Number & Opera*

10	20
30	40
50	60

McGraw-Hill Children's Publishing

0-7424-1811-1 *Number & Operations*

twenty	ten
forty	thirty
sixty	fifty

0-7424-1811-1 *Number & Operat...*

70	80
90	100
ones place	tens place

McGraw-Hill Children's Publishing

0-7424-1811-1 *Number & Operations*

eighty

seventy

one
hundred

ninety

34

34

0-7424-1811-1 *Number & Operatio*

+

−

>

<

$\dfrac{1}{2}$

$\dfrac{1}{4}$

McGraw-Hill Children's Publishing

0-7424-1811-1 *Number & Operations*

minus, subtract
2 − 1 = 1

🍎🍎 − 🍎 = 🍎

plus, add
2 + 1 = 3

🍎🍎 + 🍎 = 🍎🍎🍎

less than
1 < 2

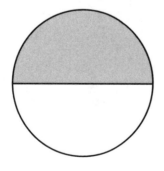

greater than
5 > 3

one half

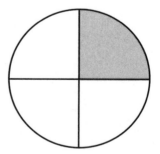

one fourth

0-7424-1811-1 *Number & Operatio*

$=$	$\dfrac{1}{3}$
sum	difference
regroup	fact family

McGraw-Hill Children's Publishing

0-7424-1811-1 *Number & Operations*

one third

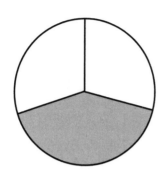

equal
5 = 5

🦢 🦢 🦢 🦢 🦢 = 🦢 🦢 🦢 🦢 🦢

Five equals five.

When you **subtract** numbers, you find the **difference**.
5 − 3 = 2
2 is the **difference**.

When you **add** numbers, you find the **sum**.
3 + 2 = 5
5 is the **sum**.

addition and subtraction problem using the same 4 numbers

3 + 2 = 5
2 + 3 = 5
5 − 3 = 2
5 − 2 = 3

To move the tens and ones.

$$\begin{array}{r} {\overset{2}{\cancel{3}}}{\overset{1}{1}} \\ -\,9 \\ \hline \end{array}$$

128

0-7424-1811-1 *Number & Operatio*